Jung and the Bible

Wayne Gilbert Rollins

John Knox Press
ATLANTA

Unless otherwise indicated Scripture quotations are from the Revised Standard Version of the Holy Bible, copyright, 1946, 1952 and © 1971, 1973 by the Division of Christian Education, National Council of the Churches of Christ in the U.S.A. and used by permission.

The Collected Works of C. G. Jung, ed. Herbert Read, Michael Fordham, Gerhard Adler, William McGuire; trans. R. F. C. Hull, Bollingen Series XX. Reprinted by permission of Princeton University Press.

MEMORIES, DREAMS, REFLECTIONS, by C. G. Jung, recorded and edited by Aniela Jaffe, translated by Richard and Clara Winston. Translation copyright © 1961, 1962, 1963 by Random House, Inc. Reprinted by permission of Pantheon Books, a division of Random House, Inc.

The author wishes to thank Mr. William McGuire of Princeton University Press for advice in identifying research materials used in the preparation of this volume.

Library of Congress Cataloging in Publication Data

Rollins, Wayne G.
  Jung and the Bible.

  Bibliography: p.
  Includes index.
    1. Bible—Criticism, interpretation, etc.—
  History—20th century. 2. Christianity—Psychology.
  3. Psychoanalysis and religion. 4. Jung, C. G.
  (Carl Gustav), 1875–1961. I. Title.
  BS500.R64   1983   220.6   82–48091
  ISBN 0–8042–1117–5

© copyright John Knox Press 1983
10 9 8 7 6 5 4 3 2
Printed in the United States of America
John Knox Press
Atlanta, Georgia 30365

To a Special Quaternity

Amanda Meizner Myerholtz   *Ethel Kamin Rollins*
Lawrence John Myerholtz   *Arthur Gilchrist Rollins*

Preface

The Bible is an utterance of the soul. So also are the creeds, the dogmas, the songs, the prayers, the rituals, the vestments, the stained-glass windows, the sermons, and the unuttered hopes of church and synagogue that have emerged consistently over the centuries, even when repressed. The soul for Jung is natively religious, and the study of the soul, the secret of the personality, is Jung's main goal.

The purpose of this volume is to explore what it means to look at Scripture as a soul book. Some of our contemporaries look at Scripture as a book of religious facts. Others see it as a book of history. The intention of this book is to look at Scripture as a treasury of the soul, that is, the testimony of our spiritual ancestors proclaiming in history and law, prophecy and psalm, gospel and epistle, genealogy and apocalypse, their experience of the holy, and drawing us and others through us into that experience.

A secondary purpose of this volume is to suggest that scriptural study today stands to benefit from the insights of psychology and psychoanalysis. Writing in a collection of essays honoring Erwin R. Goodenough in 1968, F. C. Grant, an eminent New Testament scholar, commends Goodenough for having "pointed out the value and importance, even the necessity, of the psychological interpretation of the Bible. This is a new kind of Biblical criticism," Grant writes. "The earlier disciplines are all necessary and important . . . but psychological criticism opens up a wholly new and vast, far reaching scene. . . . Beyond the historical and exegetical interpretation of the Bible lies the whole new field of depth psychology and psychoanalysis."[1]

The work of applying psychological and psychoanalytic insight to the study of Scripture has barely begun. Most of the work to date has come from the side of psychology, but we are beginning to hear stirrings from the side of biblical scholarship as well. The present volume hopes to contribute to and encourage that development.

The present work began with a graduate seminar on "Jung and the Bible" that Dr. Leighton McCutchen, Professor of Psychology and Religion, and I, as Professor of New Testament, taught at the Hartford Seminary Foundation in Fall, 1971. Its substance developed further in papers presented at various meetings of the American Academy of Religion and in a lecture series of the Ecumenical Summer Institute at Assumption College, Worcester, Massachusetts, at the invitation of Fr. Luc Martel, A.A.

I owe special thanks to Dr. Richard Ray, recent editor of John Knox Press, for endorsing the publication of this book, and to Joan Crawford, Supervising Editor of John Knox Press for expert assistance all along the way; to the members of the Broadview Community Church in Hartford, where I served as interim pastor for eight months, for the gift of an electric typewriter on which most of the drafts were done; to Mrs. Bea Charette, Mrs. Pat Dombek, and especially Mrs. Florence Fay of Assumption College for help in preparing the typescript; and to my wife Donnalou for unceasing encouragement and interest in the project.

W. G. R.
West Hartford, Connecticut

Contents

C. G. Jung Chronology'

1875   Born July 26, in Kesswil, Switzerland to Lutheran Pastor
            Johann Paul Achilles Jung (1842–1896) and Emilie, née,
            Preiswerk (1848–1923)

1895–1900   Studies medicine in Basel

1900   Decision to become a psychiatrist; appointment to staff of
            Burghölzli Mental Clinic

1902   Word association research begins, along with an extensive
            publication career that will culminate in twenty volumes of
            The Collected Works of C. G. Jung

1903   Marries Emma Rauschenbach (1882–1955); together they raise
            a family of five children, four daughters and a son; after
            re-reading Freud's *Interpretation of Dreams,* Jung begins his
            life-long research on dreams, "the most important source of
            information concerning the unconscious processes"

1905   Appointed Senior Physician at Burghölzli Clinic and lecturer
            on the Medical Faculty of the University of Zurich

1907   First meeting with Freud in Vienna

1909   Travels with Freud to Clark University, Worcester,
            Massachusetts, to receive honorary degree recognizing his
            word association experiments

1910   Appointed Permanent President of the International Congress
            of Psychoanalysis at Freud's behest

1912   Lectures on psychoanalytic theory at Fordham University

1913   Break with Freud; calls his own work "Analytical
            Psychology" rather than "Psychoanalysis;" begins his personal
            inventory of the images spontaneously produced by the
            unconscious (1913–1917), at the same time maintaining a
            large private practice

1914   World War I. Resigns Presidency of International Congress of
            Psychoanalysis; becomes captain in army medical service

1915   Intensification of research on dreams and mythology

1918   Begins study of early Christian gnosticism

1920–1927   Intermittent travel to Algiers, New Mexico, Kenya, and Egypt

1922	Purchases Bollingen property, which he uses as a life-long retreat for working with his hands and living closer to nature
1927	Focus on mandala studies
1928	First interest in alchemical texts; publication of "The Spiritual Problem of Modern Man"
1933	President, General Medical Society for Psychotherapy; first meeting of the Eranos society, to be an annual international congress on Jungian themes, at the estate of the foundress, Frau Olga Froebe-Kapteyn, in Ascona, Switzerland on Lake Maggiore
1934	Founds International General Medical Society for Psychotherapy and serves as first president
1936	Honorary degree at Harvard University; publication of "The Religious Ideas in Alchemy"
1937	Terry Lectures at Yale University on "Psychology and Religion," published in 1938
1938	Honorary doctorate at Oxford University; membership in Royal Society of Medicine; travels to India with honorary degrees at Hindu University, University of Allahabad, and University of Calcutta
1943	Honorary member, Swiss Academy of Sciences
1944	Occupies chair in Medical Psychology founded in his name at University of Basel
1945	Serious illness forces resignation from University of Basel; honorary degree at University of Geneva
1947	Retirement to Bollingen
1952	Publication of *Answer to Job*
1955	Honorary doctorate at Eidgenössische Technische Hochschule in Zurich; the citation reads: "To the man who rediscovered the wholeness and polarity of the human psyche and its tendency to integration; To the diagnostician of the symptoms of crisis in the human race in the age of science and technology; To the interpreter of primal symbolism and the process of individuation in mankind"[2]
1957	Publication of "The Undiscovered Self"
1961	Death, June 6, in Küsnacht, Switzerland; posthumous publication of *Memories, Dreams, Reflections*
1964	Publication of Jung's final essay, "Approaching the Unconscious" in *Man and His Symbols*

CHAPTER I

What Has Jung to Do with the Bible?

> I do not write as a biblical scholar (which I am not), but as a layman and physician who has been privileged to see deeply into the psychic life of many people.
>
> —*Answer to Job* [1]

Most people have heard the name of Carl Gustav Jung. Many will identify him with the field of depth psychology and others will be familiar with his theories of "archetypes" and the "collective unconscious." Still others will know that he introduced the words *extrovert* and *introvert* into popular language and taught us to think of ourselves psychologically in terms of "complexes."

I do not recall when I first heard of Jung. Most likely it was in connection with a course on the psychology of religion in divinity school, or perhaps in a bookstore coming across the beautifully illustrated hardback version of *Man and His Symbols,* which carried a large Chinese mandala in reds, greens, blues, and browns on its high-gloss dust-jacket.

In any event, it was well into my career as a professor of Biblical Studies that I developed a hunch that the life and thought of Jung had something important to say about the Bible and biblical "hermeneutics," the science of biblical interpretation. It was on the strength of that hunch, reinforced by reading and friends, that a colleague and I decided to offer a course on "Jung and the Bible" in the graduate program at the Hartford Seminary Foundation.

On the basis of what we learned in that course and subsequent research, I presented a summer lecture series to an ecumenical audience on the Assumption College campus in Worcester, Massachusetts. In the group was an artist who painted and sculpted. One of his paintings hung in a campus building. After one of the lectures he volunteered that he had begun reading Jung fifteen years ago and that he had since read the entire *Collected Works* and anything else he could find. I asked him, "Why?" and he responded, "Jung was the first person to explain to me what I was doing."

Jung often has such an effect on his readers. To some extent it was true for me. Jung had set me thinking of myself and of the psyche in more probing ways, but he had also set me thinking about Scripture from a new perspective. Jung's work had suggested a way of addressing a whole new set of questions, largely untouched by biblical scholarship, about the Bible and the role it has played in Judaeo-Christian consciousness generation after generation.

Some Unanswered Questions About the Bible

The questions that biblical scholars have conventionally addressed to the Bible have had to do with the origin, nature, and meaning of the ancient text: "When? By whom? Under what historical circumstances? For what purpose? What does it mean in the original Hebrew or Greek?" The harvest of knowledge that these questions have brought has been immense, and our insight into the meaning of the Bible and of the origin and nature of our faith communities continues to grow and be strengthened as a result.

But there are questions that biblical scholarship has left unasked, not because it doesn't want to pursue these questions, but because its method and training are not equipped to cope with them. These questions have to do not with the *origin* of Scripture but with its *effect* on the life of its readers.[2] Why, for example, is it that Scripture can have such a catalytic effect on its readers, so that a Jonathan Edwards reports he has been moved by "a new sort of affection"? Why is it that the gospel message spread with such amazing speed across the Mediterranean world, traveling from Jerusalem to Rome within two decades? Why do painters, novelists, poets, and film makers, many of them untouched by organized religion, keep returning to Scripture for their stories, heroes, and themes? What is so compelling about the Christ figure, the Psalms, even the lurid images of the Apocalypse? What is the secret of the continuing appeal of the "old, old story," generation after generation, across national and ethnic lines, touching, changing, challenging, and renewing individuals and communities? What is the peculiar attraction of the image of the rock, the serpent, the tree, the seed, the mountain, Leviathan, and the vineyard, or of the numbers 3, 5, 7, and 12, that the biblical authors keep returning to these symbols? Is the transaction between Bible and reader primarily cerebral; does it involve mostly the thinking side of the self, or are there other parts of the self at play that transcend the purely intellectual and operate at a level deeper than conscious knowledge? Is there any way biblical scholarship can inquire critically into this apparent love affair between the Bible and the human psyche? Is there a way for it to probe the mystery of the prevailing power of Scripture in the soul and to comprehend the many tongues in which it speaks to the full range of human understanding?

It appeared to me that Carl Jung was one of the few persons who was beginning to touch on such questions, with his interest in the inner workings of the human psyche, in symbol and archetype, in the key stories and key themes that appear over and over in the folk traditions of cultures around the world, dealing with the universal journey of the human soul.

The Bible in Jung's Life

An additional reason for my interest in Jung, one that I had not anticipated, was the discovery of the extensive and significant role the Bible plays in his writing and thought. In his preface to *Answer to Job*, Jung makes the statement: "I do not write as a biblical scholar (which I am not), but as a layman and physician who has been privileged to see deeply into the psychic life of many people."[3] Despite this disclaimer, Jung probably comes closer to being a scholar of the Bible than any of his peers in psychology, not only by virtue of his interest in religious texts in general, but above all by virtue of his having been raised in a biblical environment, in the family of a Swiss Lutheran clergyman. Jung writes, "In my mother's family there were six parsons, and on my father's side not only was my father a parson but two of my uncles also. Thus I heard many religious conversations, theological discussions, and sermons."[4]

Given Jung's later contact with the academic world, one might expect that a scientific approach to Scripture would have appealed to him. But as Jung was later to comment in his Terry Lectures on *Psychology and Religion* at Yale, he found the current academic study of the Bible wanting. In his experience it had done little to foster true religious feeling and insight and in many cases had seemed to forestall rather than encourage religious experience. "Nor has scientific criticism . . . been very helpful in enhancing belief in the divine character of the holy scriptures," Jung states. "It is also a fact that under the influence of a so-called scientific enlightenment great masses of educated people have either left the church or have become profoundly indifferent to it. If they were all dull rationalists or neurotic intellectuals, the loss would not be regrettable. But many of them are religious people, only incapable of agreeing with the existing forms of belief."[5]

Nor is this to say that Jung was attracted to a biblical literalism. In Jung's estimation, biblical literalism was the accidental offspring of the Protestant Reformation, which in time and in certain quarters sought to countermand papal authority with an inerrant authority of its own, namely Scripture, and with indisputable claims on its true meaning. Over against a literalistic view of Scripture, Jung was much more at home with Luther's judgment that the Bible is not to be construed as the "words" of God but as the Word of God.

Although Jung alludes to the Bible frequently throughout his writing, he rarely focuses on a biblical theme exclusively. *Answer to Job*, written in 1952, is the only work of Jung's given solely to the discussion of a biblical text.

Prior to this, Jung addressed biblical materials more or less indirectly. In 1937 he delivered the Yale Terry Lectures which touched on biblical themes. Within the next five years he wrote essays on the "dogma of the trinity" from a psychological perspective and on the "transformation symbolism in the Mass." A decade later he wrote on the fish symbol in early Christian imagery in conjunction with a major essay on "Christ, a Symbol of the Self."

Related essays that touch on the meaning and interpretation of religious texts include "Religious Ideas in Alchemy," "On the Relation of Analytical Psychology to Poetry," and three essays on Far Eastern religious texts, "The Tibetan Book of the Great Liberation," "The Tibetan Book of the Dead," and the Chinese alchemical text, "The Secret of the Golden Flower."

However, the most telling testimony to Jung's familiarity with the Bible is not to be found in the occasional essay on a biblical theme, but in the repeated allusions and references to biblical figures, phrases, images, and concepts. In the *Collected Works* one can find references to all but thirteen of the sixty-six books of the Hebrew Scriptures and the New Testament. His favorite biblical work is the fourth Gospel, which he refers to as "my beloved Gospel according to St. John,"[6] which he cites more than 120 times. In addition, Jung regularly cites passages in the intertestamental literature of the Old Testament Apocrypha and Pseudepigrapha, with references to Ecclesiasticus (Ben Sirach), the Slavonic Book of Enoch, II Esdras, Tobit, and the Wisdom of Solomon. He also shows considerable familiarity with the post-New Testament apocryphal writings, such as the Gospel of the Egyptians, the book of the Apostle Bartholomew, the Gospel of Peter, Acts of Peter, the Acts of John, the Gospel of Philip and the Acts of Thomas. Jung found several of the so-called "unknown sayings of Jesus" hidden in these extra-biblical texts of special interest. In a letter to W. R. Corti, Jung spoke of the importance of seeing oneself objectively. He cited a saying of Jesus recorded in the fifth-century Biblical Codex Bezae: "Man, if indeed thou knowest what thou doest, thou art blessed; but if thou knowest not, thou art cursed, and a transgressor of the law." In yet another context Jung quotes a saying of Jesus cited in the writings of the fourth-century church father, Origen: "He who is near me is near the fire."[7]

Biblical personalities, names, and images are regular features of Jung's writings: Adam and Eve, Abraham, Isaac, Uriah, Nicodemus, the man at the pool of Bethesda, Jonah, Hosea, along with the scapegoat, the barren fig-tree, the serpent, and the mustard seed, not to mention countless allusions to St. Paul and Jesus.

Biblical phraseology slips into the Jungian text easily and naturally. Not only such focal images as the "kingdom of God within," "*metanoia,*" or the "inner man," but also stock biblical expressions and phrases such as "white-washed sepulchres," "a wind that bloweth

where it listeth," and "a mighty rushing wind." Typical of Jung's use
of biblical phraseology is a passage in his essay, "The Father in the
Destiny of the Individual." In making the point that some parents
victimize their children because they themselves are under the control
of a father or mother archetype, Jung observes, "They do not know
that by succumbing to the compulsion they pass it on to their children
. . . 'They know not what they do.' "[8]

Jung found it intriguing when biblical figures appeared in dreams,
his own as well as those of his patients. Two of his dreams set forth
the images of Elijah, Salome, and Uriah, along with a large Bible
"bound in shiny fishskin"! Jung tells us, "Naturally I tried to find a
plausible explanation for the appearance of Biblical figures in my
fantasy by reminding myself that my father had been a clergyman."[9]
Though Jung understood that his religious upbringing undoubtedly
accounted for the presence of these images in his unconscious, he was
later to postulate that the criterion the unconscious employs in admitting a particular image into one's dreams is not necessarily the meaning the image held in its original context (in this case Jung's home or
the Bible), but rather the meaning it has taken on in the psyche of the
dreamer. The reason may be *personal,* i.e., a private meaning the
dreamer has associated with the image. Or, as Jung later suggests, the
reason may be *collective,* i.e., a meaning that tends to be associated
with such an image on a species-wide basis.

Jung's extensive use of the Bible is rooted above all in his conviction that *the Bible often speaks trenchantly to the human condition.*
When a patient writes Jung about her difficulty in searching for God,
Jung incorporates in his response a quotation from 1 Corinthians 2:10,
"The spirit searches . . . the deep things of God."[10] On another
occasion, addressing a patient who is having difficulty in facing a
darker side of himself, Jung cites the parable of the Pharisee and the
publican, in which the Pharisee, also resistant to his dark side, says,
"I thank thee Lord that I am not as this publican and sinner."[11]

Jung found *personal comfort and encouragement in the Bible.* He
cites Job 5:18 as a passage that addressed his condition helpfully at
a difficult juncture. The passage reads, "For he wounds, but he binds
up; he smites, but his hands heal." In a similar vein, Jung confided
to a friend that when he was going through one of his darkest hours,

the 35th chapter of Isaiah gave him the courage to proceed with his work. The passage opens with the words: "The wilderness and the dry land shall be glad and the desert shall rejoice and blossom."[12]

The story of Adam in the garden had also been of help to Jung early in his youth when for a period he was plagued with what he regarded as an "inconceivably wicked" and "sacrilegious" thought that forced itself upon him beyond his ability to resist. "Why," he asked, "should I have to think something inconceivably wicked? Where do such thoughts come from? After all," he debated, "I didn't create myself, I came into the world the way God made me." Pondering the Adam story, he found an analogy to his own experience. "God in his omniscience had arranged everything so that the first parents would have to sin." This seemed to be an inescapable conclusion. But, Jung asked himself, could it be that the very sins that seem almost to be written in our destinies are part of God's plan to lead us to him, even if it takes us through the fire?[13]

Jung turns so frequently to the figures of Adam, Abraham, Paul, and Christ because they represent for him, among other things, models of persons who have gone against the storm, who have responded to their call without a notion of where it would lead, who have been summoned out of Eden, Ur, Tarsus, or Nazareth to another place God would show them. Jung writes, "I recognized clearly that my path led irrevocably outward, into the limitations and darkness of three-dimensionality. It seemed to me that Adam must once have left Paradise in this manner; Eden had become a specter for him, and light was where a stony field had to be tilled in the sweat of his brow."[14] Jung himself had traveled a lonely route and he found special meaning in a New Testament apocryphal saying he frequently quoted to friends: "And where there is one alone, I say I am with him."[15]

Perhaps the most impressive evidence of the importance of the Bible for Jung is a vertical stone monument that stands by the Jung family tomb in the graveyard in Küsnacht. On the four sides of the base of this square stone adorned with the family crest is a pair of Latin inscriptions. The first is one that Jung had also inscribed over the entrance to his home. It reads: *"Vocatus atque non vocatus Deus aderit"* ("Summoned or not, God will be present"). The second, however, comes from the writings of Paul: *"Primus homo terrenus de*

terra; secundus homo coelestis de coelo" ("The first man was from the
earth, a man of dust; the second man is from heaven").[16] Though Jung
offers no commentary on what these words from 1 Corinthians 15:47
signify for him, the words themselves echo a theme found throughout
his autobiography; on the one hand people are for "this world, this
life," but on the other they are part of the eternal.

A Look Ahead

Jung was a psychologist, not a biblical scholar. Yet he had a
biblical understanding of the world. The realities and experiences that
concern him most are also those that occupy prime attention in the
writings of the biblical authors: a sense of soul, of personal destiny and
call; an openness to the wisdom of dreams, revelations, and visions;
an understanding of the power of word and image; an appreciation of
the fugue-like interplay between light and darkness; an awareness of
the reality of evil within God's world; a sense of the paradox that
where sin is great, grace abounds; and above all, the sense of God—
the numinous,[17] the holy, at the center of things.

How Jung came to appreciate Scripture and life in this way is the
subject of the chapters ahead. We will begin in chapter II with an
overview of Jung's psychology and the journey he took to arrive there:
his childhood experiences with his parents in a Swiss Lutheran par-
sonage; his choice to enter the field of psychiatry; the insights he
gleaned at the side of severely ill persons at the Burghölzli Psychiatric
Clinic in Zurich; his word-association experiments and his lifelong
dream research in pursuit of the secrets of the personality; his friend-
ship and break with Freud; his experimental descent into the unconscious; and in his maturing years, his arrival at the conclusion that
the psyche's main task, which it pursues automatically and unremit-
tingly, is its individuation or wholeness. This overview is supple-
mented by the chronological table of the key events in Jung's life on
pages viii-ix.

The remaining chapters deal with questions about Scripture that
Jung helps us consider: What does it mean to speak of ourselves as
soul and the Bible as a soul book (chapter III)? Why do we need
symbols and what role do they play in Scripture and in the life of the
soul (chapter IV)? Why does the "old, old story" continue to speak

with what Jung calls archetypal power (chapter V)? How are we to read a soul book—if that is what the Bible indeed is? How are we to mine its multileveled meanings (chapter VI)? Finally, what is the role that Scripture should play in the life of the soul in its journey before God (chapter VII)? These and other questions are raised by Jung and they bear pondering.

CHAPTER II

Jung's Psychology:
An Internal Biographical Account

> My life has been permeated and held together by one idea and one goal: namely, to penetrate into the secret of the personality. Everything can be explained from this central point, and all my works relate to this one theme.
>
> —*Memories, Dreams, Reflections*[1]

James Hillman in *Revisioning Psychology* proposes, "Each psychology is a confession, and the worth of a psychology for another person lies not in the places where he can identify with it because it satisfies his psychic needs, but where it provokes him to work out his own psychology in response."[2] In the present chapter we will explore Jung's psychology, which can, by his own acknowledgment, be seen as a confession arising out of an immense treasury of data gathered from Jung's research and personal experience.

Jung's goal, however, was not to enlist others to repeat his confession, but to encourage them to learn what they could and then press forward on their own. As he repeated to his friends and colleagues, he alone could legitimately be called a Jungian. "I do not want anybody to be a Jungian. I want people above all to be themselves."[3] What he did wish to achieve, however, was to share with as much precision as possible the truths he had known and experienced. "My own understanding is the sole treasure I possess, and the greatest. Though infinitely small and fragile in comparison with the powers of darkness, it is still a light, my only light."[4]

Jung's Father and Mother: A Dual Legacy

Jung's professional life as well as his personal life begins with his parents—his father, Johann Paul Achilles Jung, a Swiss Lutheran pastor and son of a prominent professor of surgery at the University of Basel named Carl Gustav Jung, and his mother, Emilie (née, Preiswerk) Jung, member of an established Basel family and a continuing line of theologians and clergy. Jung writes of the deep prevailing influence of his parents on the shape and direction of his life and career:

> I feel very strongly that I am under the influence of things or questions which were left incomplete and unanswered by my parents and grandparents and more distant ancestors. It often seems as if there were an impersonal karma within a family, which is passed on from parents to children. It has always seemed to me that I had to answer questions which fate had posed to my forefathers, and which had not yet been answered, or as if I had to complete, or perhaps continue, things which previous ages had left unfinished.[5]

Jung had once commented that "theology had alienated my father and me from one another."[6] Filled with questions about traditional religion and beliefs, Jung found his father reproving him: "You always want to think. One ought not to think but believe!" But Jung had responded silently within himself, "No, one must experience and know."[7]

Jung began to perceive that the religion of his father and of most everyday Christians appeared to be a "theological religion," a *doctrine about God* at the expense of the *experience of God*. Even when his father would preach on such "burning questions" as grace, his sermons sounded "stale and hollow, like a tale told by someone who knows it only by hearsay and cannot quite believe it himself."[8] In Jung's judgment, his father "had taken the Bible's commandments as his guide; he believed in God as the Bible prescribed and as his forefathers had taught him," but he did not seem to know "the immediate living God who stands, omnipotent and free, above His

Bible and His Church, who calls upon man to partake of His freedom,"[9] whose temple was the whole cosmos, ranging from the rivers and woods to "the darkness of the abyss," a God whom Jung was later to describe as an "annihilating fire and an indescribable grace"[10] in whom his personal destiny and that of all time and space was inscrutably formed.

Shortly before his father's death in 1896, Jung discovered that his father's resolute refusal to think critically about the church's dogmas and creeds and his tendency to repeat "the same old lifeless theological answers" led to grave inward doubts. On one occasion, quite by chance, Jung overheard his father in prayer, wrestling desperately to hold on to his "theological religion," which in Jung's estimation his father had tragically mistaken for faith.[11]

This experience led Jung to a lifelong interest in the relationship between orthodox profession and religious experience, seeking to demonstrate what his father tragically failed to discover, that the true object of religious faith is not a particular creed or dogma but the experienced reality to which they point. As Jung was to elaborate in his Terry Lectures at Yale some forty years later, dogma is not the end of religious faith, as helpful and necessary as it is for voicing faith's content, but the means by which the soul gives voice to "the drama of repentance, sacrifice and redemption" that takes place perennially in the human soul.[12]

However, as much as Jung found himself at odds with his father theologically, he found himself at home vocationally. Not that Jung aspired to ordination or a theological career. His father in fact had once warned Jung cryptically against this route.[13] Rather, Jung found in his father a model of "a caretaker of the Christian soul." Behind the inflexible theological facade, Jung found a "dear and generous father,"[14] a man who had done "a great deal of good—far too much,"[15] who provided Jung with a model of caring that was to inform sixty years of his own professional life. As Jung was later to observe, psychotherapy like Christianity is a "way of healing." As a psychologist Jung was able in his own way to continue his father's agenda, but in a form that Jung's father might not have recognized as originating with himself.

Jung's mother left him a complementary legacy. Unlike her hus-

JUNG

Jung's parents in 1876, Johann Paul Achilles Jung (1842-1896), a Swiss Lutheran pastor, and Emilie Jung, née, Preiswerk (1848-1923).*

Emma Rauschenbach and Jung in the year they were married (1903). A psychologist in her own right, Emma Jung did extensive research on the Holy Grail legend. Her letters to Freud are among the most insightful in the voluminous Jung-Freud correspondence.*

*C. G. Jung, *Word and Image,* ed. Aniela Jaffe, Bollingen Series 97: Vol. 2. Copyright ©1979 by Princeton University Press. Plates Nos. 9, 129, and 140 reprinted by permission of Princeton University Press. †Courtesy of Clark University Archives. ‡Courtesy of the Harvard University Archives.

Jung was invited with Sigmund Freud to lecture and receive an honorary degree at Clark University in Worcester, Massachusetts, September 1909. First row, from left, Freud, G. Stanley Hall, Jung; second row, A.A. Brill, Ernest Jones (later Freud' biographer), Sandor Ferenczi.†

Jung with his wife, Emma, and four of the five Jung children: Franz, Agathe, Marianne, and Gret at Château-d'Oex 1917.*

Jung at Harvard September 1936 on t Harvard's Tercente tion. Jung receive Doctor of Scien presented an addr logical Factors De Behavior." ‡

band, she felt no need to play the role of a professional defender of the faith, and often with a cheerful impishness played just the opposite role. Jung recalls her delight on one occasion repeating a parody she had composed of the first line of a popular church hymn she had found particularly fatuous.

More significantly, Jung's mother seemed bent on pushing Jung beyond the confines of conventional piety, introducing him as a youngster to books on the "heathen" religions of India, and as a young university student to Goethe's *Faust,* which was to feed Jung's life-long interest in the mysterious role that evil can play "in delivering man from darkness and suffering."[16]

One area in particular that can be traced to the influence of Jung's mother is his continuing interest and research in so-called spiritualis-tic or parapsychological phenomena. Though always on the periphery of his research, these phenomena continued to attract Jung's attention as worthy of empirical, psychological research.

Jung's interest in parapsychology had begun with his inaugural dissertation for the medical degree in psychiatry at the University of Zurich in 1902. Though his professors had shown little initial interest in his research, Jung eventually was able to convince them that the case study of a fifteen-year-old girl, who had experienced somnambu-listic states and had produced spiritualistic phenomena, was of schol-arly psychological interest. His dissertation, "On the Psychology and Pathology of the So-Called Occult Phenomena," analyzed two years of observations of the activities of this young girl and at the same time presented a scholarly summary and review of the entire corpus of clinical literature on somnambulism, amnesia, and hystero-epilepsy. Jung's interest in parapsychology was initially met with disbelief by friends and professional colleagues. His mother, however, offered encouragement, which in turn nourished Jung's lifelong stance of a "broad empiricism."[17]

Jung's father had tutored him in conventional faith and the art of caring for souls; his mother however had imparted to him the daring to venture beyond as well, to explore unconventional possibilities and to stand against the brick walls of traditionalist views. Jung was to combine the spiritual legacy from both in a vocational choice he made near the eve of the century year, 1900.

The Choice

Jung's past and future seemed to crystallize one day in 1899 as he was finishing his university work and preparing state examinations in medicine at Basel. Up to that point Jung had entertained several vocational options. A childhood collection of fossils, insects, minerals, and bones had led him in the direction of archaeology. But since the University of Basel had offered no courses in archaeology he selected the natural sciences, which also reflected a long-standing love for "every stone, every plant, every single thing" that seemed alive.[18]

Jung's involvement in the physical sciences was balanced by an equally vital commitment to the humanities. "Both powerfully attracted me," he reports. Between the ages of 16 and 25 he had ranged widely in theology and philosophy, from Plato, Pythagoras, and Empedocles, to Kant, Schopenhauer, and Hegel, to the mystic Eckhardt, and to Nietzsche whose thought was widely debated in university circles at the time. Committed now to the medical sciences, Jung faced the decision on a field of specialization. The choice seemed to lie between surgery and internal medicine, with a personal preference for surgery stemming from the distinguished work he had done in his studies in the fields of anatomy and pathology.

The dilemma resolved itself in the course of Jung's preparation for the examinations. He had reserved the examination in psychiatry for last. He had found the lectures in psychiatry singularly uninspiring and was not at all convinced that this discipline did not deserve the contempt it appeared to enjoy in so much of the medical world at the time. It was with reservation, therefore, that Jung picked up the *Textbook on Psychiatry* by Krafft-Ebing, wondering what a professional in the field was going to say about this controversial discipline.

> Beginning with the preface, I read, "It is probably due to the peculiarity of the subject and its incomplete state of development that psychiatric textbooks are stamped with a more or less subjective character." A few lines further on, the author called the psychoses "diseases of the personality." My heart suddenly began to pound. I had to stand up and draw a deep breath. My excitement was intense, for it had become clear to me, in a flash of illumination, that for me the only possible goal was psychiatry.[19]

Two streams of interest that up to that point in Jung's life had diverged now seemed to be converging. "Here was the empirical field common to biological and spiritual facts, which I had everywhere sought and nowhere found," Jung states. "Here at last was the place where the collision of nature and spirit became a reality."[20]

On December 10, 1900, Jung took up residence as assistant at the Burghölzli Mental Hospital in Zurich, devoting the first six months to reading all fifty volumes of the *Allgemeine Zeitschrift für Psychiatrie,* a general journal of psychiatry, to acquaint himself with the "psychiatric mentality," and then to embark on his "main business."

Jung's "Main Business"

Johann Wolfgang Goethe once spoke of his epic poem *Faust* as his "main business." Recounting his own career, Jung writes, "From my eleventh year I have been launched upon a single enterprise which is my 'main business.' My life has been permeated and held together by one idea and one goal: namely, to penetrate into the secret of the personality. Everything can be explained from this central point, and all my works relate to this one theme."[21]

The particular form this "main business" took when Jung entered the Burghölzli Clinic is expressed in a question that burned with increasing intensity in Jung's mind as he observed the depradations of mental illness firsthand: "What actually takes place inside the mentally ill?"

Until the time that Freud and then Jung introduced psychology into the discipline of psychiatry, mental illness was treated largely as a symptom of a physical ailment. Treatment was almost entirely superficial. The patient was first classified under such labels as schizophrenic, alcoholic neurasthenic, catatonic, or hallucinatory. Treatment consisted at best of narcotic depressants, and at worst of suicide prevention. When the patient deceased, slides of the patient's brain tissue were prepared for laboratory analysis.

In a flurry of articles on "A Case of Hysterical Stupor in a Prisoner in Detention" (1902), "On Manic Mood Disorder" (1903), "On Simulated Insanity" (1903), "On Hysterical Misreading" (1904), and on "The Psychology of Dementia Praecox" (1906), Jung found himself developing a new attitude toward mental illness and toward the mentally ill.

First, Jung began to suspect that the origins of mental illness may not be physical but psychic, not the function of a diseased body but the expression of a diseased personality or mind. Second, he began to suspect that the so-called symptoms of mental illness—hallucinatory and delusory language as well as compulsive behavior—were not just meaningless chaff but significant clues that might provide a key to the patient's illness and the secret behind it. "Through my work with the patients," Jung comments, "I realized that paranoid ideas and hallucinations contain a germ of meaning. A personality, a life history, a pattern of hope and desires lie behind the psychosis."[22] These hopes and desires, Jung found, are often expressed in a coded form through a particular set of words or acts, no matter how bizarre or exotic. What is needed to break the code is a physician willing to take the psychotic symptoms seriously as the specialized language of the voice of illness.

Two cases stand out in Jung's early days at the Burghölzli. The first is that of Babette, a thirty-nine-year-old woman, diagnosed by the staff physicians as "a paranoid form of dementia praecox" with "characteristic megalomania."[23] She had served as an object lesson to hundreds of medical students. Completely demented to all appearances, she was "given to saying the craziest things which made no sense at all, for example, 'I am Socrates' deputy' or 'I am a plum cake on a cornmeal bottom' or 'Naples and I must supply the world with noodles.' " Jung was intrigued with her imaginative language despite its absurdity and tried with all his might "to understand the content of her abstruse utterances."

On one occasion Jung caught a glimpse into the logic of Babette's utterances. He noticed that the examining doctors would often comment to the gallery in response to her strange babblings, "I don't know what it means," which in German is *"Ich weiss nicht was soll es bedeuten,"* to which Babette began to reply, "I am the Lorelei!" To the attending doctors the statement was nonsensical, but Jung observed with keen interest that Babette had made an associative link in her comment that had escaped the physicians; for the phrase they were using *("Ich weiss nicht was soll es bedeuten")* was the first line of a widely known song called "The Lorelei," which, incidentally, told of the sirens on the Rhine tempting passing sailors with their alluring songs to risk wrecking their ships on the rocks. What Jung began to see was that "although patients may appear dull and apathetic, or totally imbecilic, there is more going on in their minds, and more that is meaningful, than there seems to be. At bottom we discover nothing new and unknown in the mentally ill; rather, we encounter the substratum of our own natures."[24]

The second case was an older woman, seventy-five years old, who had been bed-ridden for forty years. She had been admitted to the hospital fifty years earlier. None of the staff, with the exception of a head nurse who had been there thirty-five years, could recall anything about her past. The woman was unable to speak and ate a largely fluid diet, mostly with her fingers.

When she was not eating, however, Jung discovered that "she made curious rhythmic motions with her hands and arms." Her diagnosis had been "catatonic form of dementia praecox," but for Jung it contributed little to an "understanding of the significance and origin of these curious gestures."

Jung found his answer one evening walking through the ward. "I saw the old woman still making her mysterious movements, and again asked myself, 'Why must this be?' Thereupon I went to our old head nurse and asked whether the patient had always been that way. 'Yes,' she replied. 'But my predecessor told me she used to make shoes.' "

An examination of the yellowing records of her case history brought to light an earlier entry that read: "She was in the habit of making cobbler's motions." Shoemakers of an earlier date had held the shoe between their knees and drew the thread up through the shoe in precisely the same motion this woman had been repeating for forty years. When the woman died some months later Jung attended the funeral to learn from a brother the event that had precipitated the woman's illness—a tragic love affair with a man who had been a shoemaker.

Out of these initial years at the Burghölzli, Jung was to produce the thesis that behind all psychosis and all its strange manifestations is a story. "Therapy only really begins," Jung postulated, "after the investigation of that whole personal story. It is the patient's secret, the rock against which he is shattered." The question that remained was how the physician might find a way to that secret.[25]

Words and Their Meanings

The method Jung first devised in 1902 to penetrate into the secret of the mentally ill was a word association test. Sir Francis Galton, cousin of Charles Darwin, had used the test at an earlier date in an abortive attempt to test intelligence. With a stopwatch in hand Galton would repeat a series of words to a subject who was asked in turn to respond with the first word that came to mind. Though Galton gathered a mass of data about individual response times and types of associations, he found little to constitute a valid measure of intelligence. The test, however, was of considerable interest to Jung insofar as the variations in response time might be of psychological significance in providing insight into the "associations" a given word evoked in a particular respondent.

Working at first with his patients at the Burghölzli Clinic, Jung devised a list of 100 words that collectively, but in random order, touched on most of the problems that lie behind the agenda of maladies Jung witnessed in his patients, ranging from familial, vocational, and religious problems to typical life experiences. The list typically included such words as the following:

1. head	7. ship	13. frog
2. green	8. lake	14. white
3. water	9. journey	15. house
4. singing	10. blue	16. old
5. death	11. rich	17. . . .
6. long	12. bird	

Sitting with the patient, Jung would read the words one-by-one, asking the patient to "answer as quickly as possible with the first word that occurs to you," and to answer with a *single* word rather than a phrase.[26]

The results intrigued Jung. He discovered that the average subject-response time to a given stimulus word was 1.2 seconds,[27] though in some instances there was a decided delay. Sometimes the subject might wait four or five seconds before responding or as long as a full minute. Occasionally there was a complete "block" with the patient failing to offer any response at all. When Jung would in such instances ask the patient "Why?" the answer would generally be that they could give no reason at all. In most instances, in fact, the individual was totally unaware of the delay!

Jung noted other anomalous responses. Sometimes the subject would respond with a laugh or physical twitch. On other occasions he might respond with a foreign word or phrase or perhaps simply repeat the stimulus word. In each case, as Jung began to postulate, the stimulus-word seemed to have touched on an association that set off an involuntary emotional response short-circuiting or in some instances "blacking out" the patient's normal response.

As Jung's interest and confidence in the significance of the word association test grew, he added testing apparatus to measure physiological changes in the subject's pulse or breathing rates that might possibly concur with the delayed verbal response. He also employed a psychogalvanometer which transmitted a feeble electric current through the subject's body, measuring any changes in the amount of current transmitted by the body that might take place as the subject responded to various stimulus words. The results were positive. Jung found that a delayed or anomalous response was almost invariably accompanied by a corresponding physiological change in the subject's respiration, heart, and galvanometric rate.

The news of Jung's work was received with great interest by his colleagues in Europe and America, and it was on the basis of this research that Jung was invited to join Sigmund Freud, whom Jung had first corresponded with and visited in 1906, to come to the United States to receive honorary doctorates at Clark University in Worcester, Massachusetts, in the fall of 1909.

What did Jung learn from these tests? First, he uncovered a truth that would be axiomatic for all his future research, namely, that certain words or ideas become "feeling-toned" for certain individuals conveying "an unconscious undertone that will color the idea each time it is recalled,"[28] occasionally carrying such profound associations for the individual as to trigger an overpowering emotional response.

Second, he arrived at the notion of the "psychological complex," resulting in the fact that for several years Jung's "psychology" was widely referred to as "complex psychology." The notion of the complex derived from Jung's observation that some of the words that evoked delayed responses in a patient seemed to be related to one another as a cluster or "complex" of feeling-toned words all of which seemed to point back to a common traumatic event or problematic life experience.

For example, Jung discovered with one of his patients that four individual words, spaced far apart in the word association list, had evoked highly anomalous responses. The four were *water, ship, lake,* and *swim.* In pursuing the meaning of these words for the patient, Jung was able to lead the patient to acknowledge consciously that he had been contemplating suicide by drowning. The "complex" of emotion-laden terms provided graph points on the emotional or psychological field of the patient, allowing patient and physician to identify a hitherto hidden center of anxiety.

Third, Jung made a discovery the truth of which was to impress him throughout his career—the apparent autonomy of the complexes. When a patient offered a delayed response he did so not of his own choosing. It was not a consciously dictated response but rather an unconscious and involuntary one that seemed to well up within him beyond conscious control. Thus it appeared that the feeling-toned complexes seemed to operate as a kind of second personality, independent of the individual's conscious intent and not infrequently contrary to it. As Jung expressed it, "We do not have complexes, rather complexes have us."

This momentous discovery that data on word associations could provide insight into the heart of a patient's illness led Jung to search for even more satisfactory ways of exploring the inner world of his patients, and so it was in 1903 that Jung turned, at first reluctantly, to consider dreams and their possible contribution to understanding a patient's story.

Dreams

Jung had read Freud's study on *The Interpretation of Dreams* in 1900, but had laid it aside, unable at the age of twenty-five to grasp its meaning. Three years later Jung picked the book up again. Fifty years later he praised Freud for rediscovering "dreams as the most important source of information concerning the unconscious processes."[29]

What rekindled Jung's interest in Freud's work was not only the suggestion that dreams provided as clear an insight into the heart of a patient's problems as the word association test did, but because Jung himself had begun to suspect that the hallucinatory images and the bizarre language of his schizophrenic patients might be made of the same stuff as dreams.

As with most people, Jung's curiosity about dreams, what they might mean and where they came from, had commenced in childhood. In fact, a dream he had had at the age of four proved particularly troubling. The dream had taken him in an Alice-in-Wonderland descent into a dark, stone-lined hole he came upon in the large meadow near his father's vicarage. It opened eventually into a dimly lighted rectangular chamber, at the center of which was a golden throne mounted by what he only later was to recognize as an ithyphallic figure.[30] What had perplexed Jung at the time and for a number of years afterward was why people have dreams like that. He had not willed to have such a disturbing dream. What then caused it? "Would God have sent a dream like that?" the youth asked himself. If so, why?

As a resident in psychiatry at the Burghölzli Clinic, Jung took up his interrogations once more, but with a new set of questions: "What is the significance of these strange, compensatory products my unconscious has been stimulated to create? What is the meaning of *this* particular dream appearing spontaneously at *this* particular time?" In answer, of course, Jung comments, "One might say . . . that my insight had been slowly ripening for a long time and had then suddenly broken through in a dream. And that, indeed, is what had happened. But this explanation is merely a description. The real question was why this process took place and why it broke through into consciousness."[31]

Over the next seventeen years, indeed the next half century, Jung examined some 80,000 dreams with his patients, searching for answers to the questions of where dreams and dream images come from, the meaning and origin of their story line, the apparent difference in

types of dreams, and above all the meaning of the dream process itself
in the life and development of the dreamer.

Where do dreams originate? To begin with, one must say that
dreams originate within the individual dreamer. An individual's
dreams do not come from outside oneself but originate within, appearing quite spontaneously in the dreamer's unconscious but pro-
grammed and staged by some component of the dreamer's total
psyche. Clearly they are not the *conscious* products of the dreamer;
in fact, it may be more precise to say that "the dream dreams itself
in the mind of the dreamer" than to state that "the dreamer dreams
the dream." In any event, the dream is a function and product of the
individual dreamer's psyche, as Jung expresses it. The dream is "a
theater in which the dreamer is himself the scene, the player, the
prompter, the producer, the author, the public, and the critic."[32]

As for *the origin of individual dream figures and images,* they
generally derive from the individual's everyday associations, though
often in highly edited and surrealized forms. Typical dream images
reported by dream research include the following: trees, neighbors,
deceased relatives, playing cards, water faucets, automobiles, spiders,
snakes, frogs, apes, prominent public figures such as presidents, movie
stars, and sports figures, as well as coins, swimming pools, airplanes,
and boats.

The *origin of the "story line" of the dream,* which is by far the most
significant aspect, is also to be found in the dreamer, playing out in
parabolic-like form the story of the dreamer's psychic status, touching
on the themes of conflicts, aspirations, needs, or problems being entertained in the dreamer's life, either at the conscious or unconscious
level.

Jung in time developed a *classification of dream types,* one of
which is the *initial dream,* which Jung found to occur frequently at
the beginning of analysis. The very first dream the analysand reported
very often provided a broad portrait of "the whole programme of the
unconscious" in the analysand's life at that particular time, and often
disclosed in minuscule form a preliminary insight into the "secret" or
problem that had led the person to seek therapy.[33]

A second type is the *recurrent dream,* which Jung found to be a
broadly experienced phenomenon, of persons dreaming the same

dream at intervals over the course of weeks, months, or years. Typical examples of recurrent dreams include the dream of missing a train, of flying, of failing an examination, of being caught before an audience with no clothes or without notes, of discovering a new and hitherto unknown room in one's house, of being chased by a dark figure, of driving a car that is somehow out of control, of being lost in a large building, and so forth.

Less common, but substantially attested is the *anticipatory dream,* also called more recently the *ESP dream,* which seems to adumbrate an event that will take place in the dreamer's future. Jung made no claims of understanding such coincidences, but found them widely enough attested to warrant scientific notice and more serious attention by the psychological researcher.

A fourth type is the *lucid dream* reported by artists, musicians, philosophers, poets, scientists, and playwrights, who report that the resolution to a problem they were currently attempting to solve in their work appeared in a dream, or that an idea for a new artistic or scientific project would appear in a dream. For example, when the nineteenth century chemist Kekulé was wrestling with the riddle of the molecular structure of benzene, he had a dream of a snake with its tail in its mouth, suggesting to Kekulé the correct solution, the closed carbon ring. Robert Louis Stevenson, long in search of a story that would portray man's double being, first encountered Dr. Jekyll and Mr. Hyde in a dream, as Samuel Taylor Coleridge also first saw Kubla Khan in a dream. As subsequent research has disclosed, Descartes, Goethe, Tolstoy, Schumann, and Wagner all drew on their dreams in their work.

A fifth type, the *big dream* or *great dream,* Jung first encountered in his visit among the Elgonyi tribe of East Africa, where the dreams of witch doctors, chieftains, and medicine men were regarded as matters of public scrutiny for the significance they might hold for the life and destiny of the entire community. John Neihardt's classic study, *Black Elk Speaks,* reports the same phenomenon among the Oglala Sioux. One recalls the seriousness with which the Pharaoh's dreams were taken in the Joseph story and perhaps, in related fashion, the "dream" of the Rev. Martin Luther King, Jr., in our own time.

Observing the role of dreams in the psychic life of his patients,

Jung began to look with renewed appreciation at the dream-lore to be found in the Bible and in classical antiquity. The Talmudic rabbis had averred that an uninterpreted dream was like an unopened letter. The author of Job wrote that "in a dream, in a vision of the night when deep sleep falls upon men, while they slumber in their bed," God "opens the ears of men, and terrifies them with warnings, that he may turn man aside from his deed" (Job 33:15–17), just as the author of Acts witnesses to a new age of revelation in which young men would see visions and old men would dream dreams (Joel 2:38; Acts 2:17), echoing the medieval conviction that *somnia a Deo missa*—"dreams are sent by God." In light of this, Jung found it ironic that so many theologians and clergy viewed his interest in dreams with such disbelief and disinterest.

One of the key hypotheses Jung proposed about dreams was that they served a constructive, compensatory function in the psychic development of the individual. Freud had taken the dream to be a portrait, in intentionally disguised form, of the repressed contents of the unconscious; but Jung saw other objectives on the agenda of the dream-producing mechanism in the human psyche. In the words of Joseph Campbell, "Dreams, in Jung's view, are the natural reaction of the self-regulating psychic system, and, as such, point forward to a higher, potential health. . . . The posture of the unconscious is compensatory to consciousness, and its productions, dreams, and fantasies consequently are not only corrective but also prospective, giving clues" to the direction in which the psyche at present is pressing for the self to go.[34]

Jung cites an example of the *compensatory function* of dreams in his Terry Lectures at Yale in 1937, concerning a highly intelligent scientist who had come to Jung for help. A Roman Catholic by education, he had long since abandoned the practice of his faith and admitted to no interest whatsoever in religion, and was "one of those scientifically minded intellectuals who would be simply amazed if anybody should saddle them with religious views of any kind." Yet of the 400 dreams he shared with Jung, seventy-four of them dealt explicitly and elaborately with religious motifs. Following a lengthy analysis of several of these dreams, Jung proposes that, though the man had abandoned religion at the conscious level, his unconscious had continued to find it important.[35]

This compensatory function of the psyche, according to Jung, is to be found also in the imaginative functions of the psyche related to dreams, in the art, poetry, fables, and myths that emerge, often spontaneously, from the depths of the self. Jung provides an example in the story of one of his patients, a young autoscopic girl.

When Jung had begun working with the young girl he had inquired of her previous doctors whether there was any hope for a cure. They had answered in the negative. Jung, however, proceeded with his treatment and started the girl drawing and painting. One picture she painted, Jung tells us, "showed the girl holding an open cage in her right hand as though to invite a bird, flying above, to return to the cage." Jung continues, "She is doing just what the medicine men do in Africa—open the cage at night so that the souls which escape in the night may be caught and restored to their owners. This is a beautiful picture," Jung proposes, "and shows that something might be done." The girl was in fact healed. The painting, in Jung's interpretation, was the voice of the unconscious depths of the psyche, longing for and anticipating a psychic wholeness that was not yet realized or known to conscious experience.[36]

On the basis of his lifelong research on the role of dreams in the lives of his patients, Jung was to conclude that dreams provided "even more information about the content of a neurosis" than the association test, revealing the same conflicts and complexes uncovered by them, but in a more graphic and ample measure. For Jung the dream was a kind of X-ray of the psychic state of a person, "a little hidden door in the innermost and most secret recesses of the soul,"[37] not as it could be or as the dreamer would like it to be, *"but as it is,"*[38] providing the dreamer and the analyst with the first sightings of the "rock" on which the patient may have been broken—his secret—but also pointing a way out.

With his interest whetted, Jung made the decision to follow the path that his dream research had opened up for him. He decided to make a somewhat risk-filled descent into the depths of his own unconscious in an attempt to measure its dimensions and to map as clearly as possible the uncharted hinterland of the psyche, knowing that he could not be of help to his patients unless he came to know and understand the fantastic and puzzling images that so often dominated and tyrannized their consciousness. His decision coincided with a break with Freud that was to bring into clearer definition the characteristic lines of his own psychology.

The Break with Freud

Three years after their first correspondence in 1906, Freud had confided to Jung his desire to adopt him "as an eldest son," anointing him as "successor" and "crown prince." Indeed, it was in 1910, at the urging of Freud, that Jung became Permanent President of the International Congress of Psychoanalysis, a post he was to resign after his break with Freud in 1913.

Two fundamental differences between his position and Freud's became clear to Jung in a conversation the two of them had had at the Second Congress of the Association of Psychoanalysis in 1910. Freud had entreated Jung "never to abandon the sexual theory. This is the most essential thing of all. You see," Freud went on to say, "we must make a dogma of it, an unshakable bulwark." In some astonishment Jung asked, "A bulwark—against what?" Freud replied, "Against the black tide of mud"—and then he added—"of occultism."[39] The two premises at issue were Freud's theory of sexuality and Freud's attitude toward what he had called "occultism," which Jung interpreted to mean his own avid interest in philosophy, religion, and the newer psychological interest in parapsychology.

The decisive blow came in 1912 with the publication of Jung's two-volume study on *Symbols of Transformation*. So certain was Jung in the process of writing this work that it would cause an irreparable breach between Freud and himself that for two months he was unable to put his pen to the paper. Surmounting the fear eventually, Jung proceeded with its publication, which manifested a departure from Freud on two major points.

First, Jung proposed a new theory of the libido or psychic energy which struck at the central role Freud had attributed to sexuality in the dynamics of the psyche. Freud had understood the libido primarily as a manifestation of instinctual drives: hunger, aggression, and sexuality. Jung, however, began to see the libido in terms of a more general psychic energy, comparable to physical energy, which could appear in many forms, sometimes in sexuality, to be sure, but also in the work of art, politics, religion, myth, fantasy, and dream, and could effect creative and constructive achievements in the individual as well as blindly instinctual forms of behavior.

Second, Jung began a landmark investigation into the myths and fantasies of world religion, the so-called "occult." Plowing through a mountain of mythic materials—Babylonian, American Indian, Gnostic, Hindu—Jung began to suspect affinities between the substance of these ancient myths and the modern dreams and hallucinations of his patients, and furthermore to explore the heuristic and constructive function they served in the life of the psyche as other than the negative and repressed contents of the unconscious of which Freud spoke.

The Descent into the Unconscious

Following the break with Freud, accompanied by a long period of disorientation and uncertainty for Jung, he made the decision to engage in his own personal *descensus ad inferos*, a descent into the depths of his own unconscious to discover what the "myth" was by which he was living and to come to understand better the fantasies that stirred within him as well as in his patients. Jung recounts that he "felt not only violent resistance to this, but a distinct fear," but he saw there was no other way to come to an understanding of these underground products of the psyche than by letting himself "plummet down into them" to encounter them directly.[40]

So it was between the years 1912 and 1917 he left his University post, as he expressed it, in order to devote himself full time "in the service of the psyche," though at the same time maintaining balance in his life with his private professional practice and with the family routine at "228 Seestrasse," a routine Jung deemed necessary as a "counterpoise to that strange inner world" he was exploring.[41]

The method he developed was to chronicle every single image he encountered, in his own dreams and fantasies as well as in those of his patients. His goal was to try to understand "every item of my psychic inventory, and to classify them scientifically—so far as this was possible—and, above all, to realize them in actual life. This is what we usually neglect to do. We allow the images to rise up, and maybe we wonder about them, but that is all. We do not take the trouble to understand them, let alone draw ethical conclusions from them."[42]

Jung's research records during these years initially consisted of what he called his "Black Book" and his "Red Book." The Black Book contained the written notes and observations on his experiences; the Red Book contained pictorialized depictions of them in paintings and sketches.

The particular images he recorded were as diverse and as unusual as might be expected. Some of them related to childhood experience —playing with building blocks, constructing houses and castles, early dreams. Jung was impressed with the strong feeling tone he still associated with some of these memories, that "there is still life in these things."[43] As Jung persisted in letting the images emerge in free-association patterns from his unconscious, he encountered a stream of images, surrealistic in quality, but not at all foreign to dreams and fantasies; for example: a golden chair, a speaking white dove, a dark cave, significant numbers, dwarfs, a red sun, blood, rainfall, the edge of a precipice, death; the dead coming to life, an old man with white beard accompanied by a beautiful but blind young girl, a black serpent, an emerald table. The list was endless and seemed one of a piece with those images he might find in the mythopoetic expressions of *Faust,* of Nietzsche's *Thus Spake Zarathustra,* in the biblical apocalypses, as well as in the "fund of unconscious images which fatally confuse the mental patient."

Though Jung in general found his graphic notes in the Red Book less helpful in providing an objective description of the psyche than the standard written notes of the Black Book, he did find one particular graphic form of great help in providing insight into the nature of the psyche, namely the *mandala.* The term *mandala* derives from the Sanskrit and means literally "circle." A simple and classic form of the *mandala* is a circle superimposed on a square. In oriental art the image of the *mandala* is taken as a representation of the cosmos, and consists, in more elaborate form, of any arrangement of concentric geometric shapes, ranging from triangles, circles, and squares, to crosses, wheels, and flowers.

Jung found himself fascinated with *mandalas* for two reasons. First, they were universal. They seemed to be found around the world in thousands of variations, functioning as an image to which "doodlers" as well as serious artists seem naturally drawn and which they seem to reproduce quite spontaneously on stone monuments, silk weavings, floor tiles, in textile designs and carpet patterns. Second, Jung observed in drawing *mandalas* of his own in a notebook on a daily basis that the virtually endless variety of *mandala* images his psyche seemed to produce in a period of years, from 1916 to 1927, seemed to correspond both in variety and form to the various frames-of-mind with which he had drawn them. It was as if in these drawings, as Jung comments, "I could observe my psychic transformations from day to day,"[44] and that the *mandalas* were "cryptograms" of the self.

Writing some fifty years later, Jung looked back at this risk-filled period when he was setting out on his own and pursuing his inner images as the most important in his life. "All my works, all my creative activity, has come from those initial fantasies and dreams which began in 1912."[45] Although it took him forty-five years to distill the meaning from the data he gathered at that time, he regarded all his later work as nothing more than "supplements and clarifications" of those original explorations into the psyche which provided him with the *"prima materia* for a lifetime's work."[46]

The Anatomy of the Psyche

Joseph Campbell refers to the years 1913–1946 as the master period in Jung's life, the period of the scholar-physician in which Jung began to construct a hypothesis concerning the nature and the structure of the psyche, which he postulated has both a conscious and unconscious dimension, the conscious sector constituting merely the tip of the psychic iceberg.

Consciousness is defined by Jung as that part of the psyche that is directly knowable. At its center is the archetypal complex called the "ego" or the "I" that generally regards itself in charge of the self during waking hours, receiving and screening data, monitoring emotions, feelings, and intuitions that from time to time invade consciousness, and in general planning and organizing the self's day.

Jung proposed that *consciousness* in the psyche has four main functions: the *thinking function,* concerned with objectivity and rationality; the *feeling function,* sensitive to the value or agreeableness of things; the *sensing function,* attentive to the feel, taste, sound, smell, and appearance of things; and the *intuitive function* that ponders the "whence," "whither," and "why" of things. Furthermore, Jung observed that as the ego develops in the first half of life it tends to embrace one of these functions as its *dominant* mode of operation. Two of the other functions are only partially utilized and one is in a state of almost total neglect, so that one can be characterized as being fundamentally either a "thinking," "feeling," "sensing," or "intuitive" *type*.

Jung also found that consciousness can be characterized in terms of *attitude*, the *attitude of extraversion* or the *attitude of introversion*. In the case of the former, one's libido or psychic energy tends to move outward from the self; in the latter, the energy tends to flow inward.

In 1921 essay on "Psychological Types," Jung spelled out these attitudinal and functional differences in the ego. He also added the observation that one's *psychological type* tends to shift in the second half of life, when those "functions" and the "attitude" one found most adaptive in youth, adolescence, and young adulthood are compensated for by an "attitude" and "functions" one had hitherto left undeveloped.

In an essay in the eighth volume of his *Collected Works* entitled "The Structure and Dynamics of the Psyche," Jung offers a helpful and succinct description of his understanding of the *unconscious:*

> . . . everything of which I know, but of which I am not at the moment thinking; everything of which I was once conscious but have now forgotten; everything perceived by my senses, but not noted by my conscious mind; everything which, involuntarily and without paying attention to it, I feel, think, remember, want, and do; all the future things that are taking shape in me and will sometime come to consciousness: all this is the content of the unconscious.[47]

Far from being a mere repository of forbidden thoughts, repressed desires, and lost memories, Jung sees the *unconscious* in its furthest reaches as that genetic, spiritual, and even cosmic matrix, interlaced with the special racial, tribal, familial, and personal history peculiar to each one of us, from which we emerge and out of which we live day by day, in ways that seem beyond simple conscious definition.

In Jung's judgment *the unconscious* can be understood in terms of two rather distinct dimensions which he calls the *personal unconscious* and the *collective unconscious*.

The *personal unconscious* in Jung's thought (which corresponds to the totality of the unconscious as it is understood in Freud's thinking) consists of material that relates more or less closely to one's personal life, such as ideas and sense impressions temporarily lost to memory (Freud's "preconscious") as well as feelings and thoughts too objectionable to the conscious mind to acknowledge consciously and therefore "repressed" (Freud's "subconscious").

The *collective* or *universal unconscious*, on the other hand, consists of material more remote from individual, personal experience and related more to the *collective* or to *general* human experience. Jung formulated the concept of the collective unconscious over the course of many years. He puzzled over the varied contents emerging from the unconscious, some of which seemed clearly personal, but others of which seemed to transcend the personal experience of the individual and to relate, instead, to images and patterns produced in cultures that might be centuries or continents away. For example, a modern scientist reported to Jung a series of numerical dream images which bore remarkable resemblance to alchemical writings of four hundred years earlier with which the man had had no previous contact. Likewise a ten-year-old girl, the daughter of a psychiatrist friend of Jung, reported the exotic image of four cosmic forces converging in the center from the four corners of the world, an image that is to be found in slightly modified form in a childhood dream of an Oglala Sioux medicine man. Likewise, a mental patient in a Zurich hospital reported to Jung his fantasy of a tube-like image hanging down from the sun giving birth to the wind, a figure Jung was to encounter in almost the exact words in an esoteric text in a language foreign to the patient.

On the basis of clinical data and research in comparative mythology, Jung proposed that the unconscious consists not "only of originally conscious contents that have got lost," but also has "a deeper layer of the same universal character as the mythological motifs which typify human fantasy in general." These motifs, Jung went on to say, "are not *invented* so much as *discovered;* they are typical forms that appear spontaneously all over the world, independently of tradition, in myths, fairytales, fantasies, dreams, visions, and the delusional systems of the insane."[48]

Jung revived the ancient Gnostic term *archetype* in connection with this phenomenon, not to refer in specific to the mythic figures and motifs individually repeated across cultures, but rather to the *"patterning tendency" in the human psyche to produce such images* as conventional expressions, as it were, of common human experiences. For example, no matter where one turns in world literature one finds such familiar *archetypal images* as the king, the sacred child, the prince and princess, the wise old man, the father, the evil giant, the sacred marriage, the holy man, the sacred rock, the brave young boy, the wicked witch, the wise old woman, the magic potion, the invincible weapon, the wandering hero, speaking animals, the after-life, the golden age, and the great journey. Though the specific "archetypal images" will vary in detail from culture to culture, they will be recognizable as manifestations of a *common archetype* or *archetypal pattern* that the psyche tends to revert to when it wishes to depict certain common human experiences.

Jung compares this archetypal or patterning tendency in the human species to the nest-building instinct of birds or the migratory instincts of the Bermuda eel, as well as to the physical tendency in crystals to shatter along anticipated lines dictated by an internal, molecular pattern. In similar fashion, when the human psyche is "struck" by a particular human experience, it tends to populate its stories about that experience with a "cast of inevitable stock figures that have played through all time, through the dreams and myths of all mankind, in ever-changing situations, confrontations, and costumes."[49]

Jung traces this archetypal tendency to the biological and psychological history of the race. He comments that, "just as the human body represents a whole museum of organs, each with a long evolutionary history behind it, so we should expect to find that the mind is organized in a similar way."[50] In fact, the phenomenon is written so deeply into the unconscious, according to Jung, that "one could almost say that if all the world's traditions were cut off at a single blow, the whole mythology and the whole history of religion would start all over again with the next generation."[51]

Though, to be sure, Jung affirms repeatedly that *consciousness* is "our most important weapon" for assessing, planning, determining, and shaping our lives, the fundamental discovery he made in these early years was that consciousness cannot mature or do its job properly without awareness of its roots in and relation to the unconscious. Not understanding the unconscious and not listening to the truths it knows about us as individuals and as a species and not giving audience to its "wisdom," which is more ancient and often wiser than that of the "ego," is to be deprived of one of our most valuable resources.

Jung observed the many ways in which the unconscious attempts to inform, guide, or raise the consciousness of the ego. It can create a neurosis to wake us up to onesidedness in behavior. It can trip up our speech or our memories, signalling how strong our feelings are or how confused our judgments are about certain persons or situations. It can produce the material of poetry, philosophy, religion, psychology, or even scientific insight. It can goad the conscience. And, at critical junctures in life, when consciousness seems incapable of making an intelligent decision, it can provide a path known only at the gut level that in the end will seem the best route to have taken.

The question that remained for Jung, after arriving at a portrait of the psyche that seemed to satisfy the facts, and after discovering the importance of the dialogue between consciousness and the unconscious for psychic growth, was "Where was it all leading?" What is the *raison d'être* of the psychic process? What is its goal? A clue to an answer came between the years 1919–45, when Jung turned his attention with renewed interest to the writings of the first and second century Christian Gnostics and the medieval alchemists.

Gnostics and Alchemists

Jung's study of the Gnostics between 1918 and 1926 was motivated in part by the rather odd emergence of intellectual-religious groups in the 1920s who identified themselves as "gnostic." It was also motivated by his desire to learn more about the meaning that might lurk behind the mysterious language of the Gnostic texts, which spoke of the mythic descent of the soul to earth, its reascent through the seven heavens to the realm of the Divine Pleroma or Fullness, and of the cosmic powers of the Aeons, the Demiurge, Ogdoads, and Achamoth. Jung had seen the similarities of this exotic Gnostic language to the bizarre utterances of his patients almost immediately.

Both seemed to derive from that common repository of mytho-poetic language located in the unconscious, and, as Jung comments, "This is exactly what the human psyche produces and always has produced."[52] But Jung's question was what it meant. Was there any similarity between what he as a twentieth century analytical psychologist might see in the Gnostic story and what the Gnostics themselves saw in it?

The answer to the question could, of course, never be resolved with absolute certainty. But a letter from the noted Sinologist, Richard Wilhelm, was to start Jung off in a direction that would lead to an answer that seemed to provide more insight than any theory to date into the abstruse myths of the Gnostics.

The letter from Wilhelm arrived in 1928, along with a copy in translation of an ancient Chinese alchemical text called *The Secret of the Golden Flower.* In the letter Wilhelm had invited Jung to write a commentary on the text. Jung's interest in Chinese literature had been kindled by Wilhelm's lecture on the *I Ching,* which he had offered in Zurich at Jung's invitation five years earlier. Jung decided to comply and to engage in his first serious study of the strange runes of the alchemists and their quixotic search for the elixir that would enable them to transmute common matter into gold.

Jung's first move was to notify a Munich bookseller to inform him of any medieval alchemical texts he might have available. For more than a decade Jung poured over such works—the *Artis Aurifera Volumina Duo* or the *Rosarium Philosophorum*—intrigued with the meaning of this "unknown language," compiling a lexicon of thousands of those alchemical terms that for reasons yet unknown to him were repeated time and again, such as *"unum vas"* ("the one vessel"), *"prima materia"* ("primordial matter"), *"massa confusa"* ("chaos"), and the *"lapis philosophorum"* (the "philosoper's stone," a central image that seemed to symbolize both the key and the goal of the alchemical process).

Jung had dipped into alchemical texts as early as 1914, when he had corresponded with Herbert Silberer with respect to his book on *Hidden Symbolism of Alchemy and the Occult Arts.*[53] Though he had found some of Silberer's theories on the meaning of alchemical symbolism suggestive, he had tended to dismiss the whole as "off the beaten track." But now, at Richard Wilhelm's invitation, and with his questions on Gnosticism still hanging fire, Jung took up Silberer's quest once again in a research venture that would culminate twenty-seven years later in 1955 with the publication of *Mysterium Coniunctionis* in which Jung sums up his thoughts on alchemy and the insight it provided into what he calls the "central concept" of his psychology.

What Jung gradually came to see, as he turned the stones of alchemical language in his hand day after day, noting the history of its two-edged philosophic-scientific symbolism, was that the subject matter was not *one* but *two* separate processes. To be sure, one of the processes described was clearly physical, aimed at the transmutation of base matter into gold, but the second, hidden in the philosophic overtones of alchemical symbolism, was psychic and personal, aimed at the transmutation of the self. Though dealing on the surface with alembics and crucibles, the interior subject matter of alchemy was the fusion of the base and noble components of the self through mixing, trying, and testing, into a purged and refined form. Jung began to perceive that the elaborate system of this ancient physical discipline, which in time was to father modern chemistry, was at the same time nothing less than a projection on physical substances of a process that at heart dealt with the self. It was consonant with the poetic observation of the ancient sage, that "the crucible is for silver, and the furnace is for gold, and the LORD tries hearts" (Proverbs 17:3). As Jung recalls in his autobiography:

> Only after I had familiarized myself with alchemy did I realize that the unconscious is a *process,* and that the psyche is transformed or developed by the relationship of the ego to the contents of the unconscious. In individual cases that transformation can be read from dreams and fantasies. In collective life it has left its deposit principally in the various religious systems and their changing symbols. Through the study of these collective transformation processes and through understanding of alchemical symbolism I arrived at the central concept of my psychology: *the process of* individuation.[54]

Individuation and the Self

In 1928, in an essay on "The Relations Between the Ego and the Unconscious," Jung penned an initial definition of "individuation." He states that by "individuation" he means "becoming an 'individual,' and, insofar as 'individuality' embraces our innermost, last and incomparable uniqueness, it also implies becoming one's own self."⁵⁵ Jung frequently offered the advice, "Don't imitate!" He also often reported his deep impression of "how enormously different people's psyches are."⁵⁶ The life process he saw at work in the development of the human psyche aimed precisely in that direction, not to produce a general, homogenized humanity, but rather the inimitably different and unique individuals each of us is and was meant to be.

Jung saw the process as "automatic" in that it reflects an inherent and irrepressible bent in the individual psyche toward wholeness. "Everything living strives for wholeness,"⁵⁷ Jung comments, so that one might say that the individuation process is "the expression of . . . a biological process . . . by which every living thing becomes what it was destined to be from the beginning."⁵⁸ To be sure, the individual can either frustrate or assist the process, but one can neither initiate nor stop it. It happens of itself.

Jung saw a basic principle at work in the process of individuation that he calls *enantiodromia.* Derived from the Greek, it means "the tendency toward the opposite" (*enantios* = "opposite"; *dromos* = "running toward"), which the ancient philosopher Heraclitus saw operative throughout nature and which Jung had witnessed as a manifest trait of the human psyche. "If anything of importance is devalued in our conscious life and perishes—so runs the law—there arises a compensation in the unconscious."⁵⁹ Individuation accordingly is the expression of that lifelong tendency in the human psyche to differentiate and integrate those aspects of the self that have at an earlier date either been devalued or have "perished" from conscious life.

Jung observed that the process took place in two *stages,* one commencing with birth extending to mid-life, with the second, completing stage beginning approximately between the ages of 35 to 45.

In the *first stage of individuation,* extending from birth to mid-life, the psyche's main task is the formation and consolidation of the "ego," or the "ego complex," as Jung also refers to it. Moving from the "undifferentiated unconscious wholeness" of earliest infancy, the psyche gradually develops its individual sense of "I-ness," which in turn also fashions a social self, what Jung calls the *persona* or personality, which is that part of the self the ego sees fitting in its own way to disclose readily to others. At the same time the ego is experimenting as to which *attitude* (introversion or extroversion) and which *function* (thinking, feeling, sensing, intuiting) seem best suited for adapting to the particular environment. The final tasks of this stage involve choosing a vocation, gathering a spouse, and building a family nest, all part of the demanding business of identifying oneself and one's place in the objective world.

In the *second stage of individuation,* which commences somewhere in mid-life and which occupies the bulk of Jung's professional attention, the psyche's main task is "coming to know one's other side" that has been left relatively undeveloped in the first half of life, as well as to develop a new center for the psyche which Jung calls "the Self." Questions, ideas, perspectives, and reflections that played only a passing role in the first stage now come to the fore. Sides of the self undeveloped earlier now seem, even if in a weak voice, to call for attention. Now the "thinking types" often begin to discover the need for making value judgments, or "intuitive types" may rediscover the wholeness and goodness of the physical and sensate. Attitudes toward life one has regarded as "established" and "functional" are subtly called into question, not in the sense that one has been completely wrong about these things in the past, but that one has failed to see them against the background of a larger truth. Whereas in the past many key issues in politics, religion, work, and values seemed "black and white," one now finds oneself tolerating ambiguities and entertaining polarities that one's "younger" ego would have found little patience with.

On the more deeply personal and internal side, one also begins to see oneself in more direct light, or as June Singer has expressed it in her description of the Jungian analytic process in *Boundaries of the Soul,* one begins to "look under the hood." At an earlier date this might have been distracting if not troubling. But at this point in life one feels drawn to confront the full range of one's feelings, thoughts, and desires more honestly and discerningly. One feels the need to come to a firmer understanding of all that is at work within, from the contra-sexual ingredients in one's psychic life (which Jung refers to as the *anima* in men and the *animus* in women) to the dark side or *"shadow"* that is so essential for consciousness to recognize.

The goal of the individuation process is the emergence of the Self, a term Jung uses technically to refer to that fuller self that comes into play as one begins to explore "one's other side" in the second stage of individuation.

The Self represents the totality of all that we are as individuals. It is the "completest expression" of our individuality when all its dimensions are fully considered. It is the "totality of the human psyche," the "whole circumference which embraces all the psychic phenomena" in ourselves, "our body and its workings and the unconscious," the sensate and intuitive, the intellectual and moral, the masculine and feminine, the sinister and benign. It represents all that we are, all that we were, and all that we might become, in addition to that invisible psychic and genetic "household" of ancestors and progeny in whose life and destiny we participate in ways that are only dimly felt and recognized.[60]

In the second half of life the Self tends to replace the ego as the *center of personality.* It is a center no longer rooted in the "petty, oversensitive, personal world of the ego" with its preoccupation with egotistic wish-conflicts, but "in the wider world of objective interests."[61] In a sense it is a center that is "everywhere and whose circumference is nowhere,"[62] for it finds itself at home in that broad totality of the Self, whose mysteries can never be fully plumbed but whose promptings are clearly felt. As Jung writes, the person who has found this new center is as removed from one who has not as "the man whose sun still moves around the earth is essentially different from the man whose earth is a satellite of the sun."[63]

A definitive characteristic of the Self is its sense of being *in relation,* both with others and with the historical-cultural stream of which we are part. "Coming to one's Self," Jung maintains, involves a simultaneous coming to the "conscious acknowledgement and acceptance of our kinship with those around us. Because relationship to the self is at once relationship to our fellow man, and no one can be related to the latter until he is related to himself . . . neither can exist without the other."[64] It also involves a conscious acknowledgment of our relatedness to the longer fate and history of the society and culture in which an individual lives. "Although we human beings have our own personal life," Jung writes, "we are yet in large measure the representatives, the victims and promoters of a collective spirit whose years are counted in centuries."[65] We are not, as we so often think, "only the passive witnesses of our age, and its sufferers, but also its makers."[66]

The relationship of the Self to history constituted a central theme in Jung's thought. He returns to it repeatedly in a succession of essays over the course of thirty-three years, prior to and following World War II. Gathered in the tenth volume of the *Collected Works* under the title *Civilization in Transition,* they include: "The Spiritual Problem of Modern Man" (1928); "The Meaning of Psychology for Modern Man" (1933); "Wotan," an essay on the German nationalist spirit (1936); "After the Catastrophe" (1945); "The Fight with the Shadow," first presented as a BBC broadcast (1946); "The Undiscovered Self" (1957); and the closing section of his last essay, "Approaching the Unconscious" (1961).

Jung identifies the crisis in the modern Western world as at root a crisis in the human soul:

> The gigantic catastrophes that threaten us today are not elemental happenings of a physical or biological order, but psychic events. To a quite terrifying degree we are threatened by wars and revolutions which are nothing other than psychic epidemics. . . . Instead of being at the mercy of wild beasts, earthquakes, landslides, and inundations, modern man is battered by the elemental forces of his own psyche.[67]

The Age of Enlightenment taught us that reason would overcome the human tendency to destroy others and oneself; but in fact, Jung avers, this may be our "greatest and most tragic illusion."[68] We must ask ourselves, Jung suggests, "how it is that, for all our progress in the administration of justice, in medicine and in technology, for all our concern for life and health, monstrous engines of destruction have been invented which could easily exterminate the human race."[69] The irony, Jung adds, is that these "devilish engines" are invented by "reasonable, respectable citizens" who, in many respects, are "everything we could wish."

Where can a change be found? "Our rationalistic attitude leads us to believe that we can work wonders with international organizations, legislation, and other well-meant devices." In addition, "there are well-meaning theologians and humanitarians who want to break down the power principle—in others." But, Jung insists, "we must begin by breaking it in ourselves. Then the thing becomes credible."[70] "The psychopathology of the masses is rooted in the psychology of the individual," Jung was convinced,[71] and "if the individual is not truly regenerated in spirit, society cannot be either, for society is the sum total of individuals in need of redemption."[72] What is required is "a complete spiritual renewal."[73]

In his last essay on "Approaching the Unconscious," which he completed shortly before his death in 1961, Jung made this appeal:

> As any change must begin somewhere, it is the single individual who will experience it and carry it through. The change must begin with an individual; it might be any one of us. Nobody can afford to look around and to wait for somebody else to do what he is loath to do himself. But since nobody seems to know what to do, it might be worthwhile for each of us to ask himself whether by chance his or her unconscious may know something that will help us.[74]

For Jung, the "individual human being" was "that infinitesimal unit on whom a world depends, and in whom, if we read the meaning of the Christian message aright, even God seeks his goal."[75]

CHAPTER III

The Bible and
the Life of the Soul

> . . . the general undervaluation of the human soul is so great that neither the great religions nor the philosophies nor scientific rationalism have been willing to look at it twice.
> —*Man and His Symbols*[1]

> I would go a step further and say that the statements made in the Holy Scriptures are also utterances of the soul. . . .
> —Preface, *Answer to Job*[2]

In *Insearch: Psychology and Religion,* James Hillman laments that *soul* has fallen into disuse, not only among psychologists, but among some religionists and the average man and woman as well:

> As a term . . . [the word "soul"] . . . has all but vanished from contemporary psychology; it has an old-fashioned ring, bringing echoes of peasants on the Celtic fringes or reincarnating theosophists. Perhaps it is still kept alive as some vestigial organ by village vicars and by seminary discussions of patristic philosophy. But it barely enters popular songs—who longs with "heart and soul"? Who puts his whole soul into anything? What girl has "soulful" eyes, what man a "great soul," what woman is a "good old soul"? "Soul" is the last four-letter word left that is unmentionable among the "in."[3]

As convincing as Hillman's observation seems to be, there is some evidence that *soul* is not a completely dead word. In fact, there are occasions when it carries considerable weight and when no other word in the language provides a suitable substitute.

For example, one wonders how Stephen Vincent Benet might have talked about the pact between the devil and Daniel Webster without speaking of the temptation to sell one's "soul" for a price. None of us has difficulty in empathizing with the Psalmist when he inquires, "Why are you cast down, O my soul, and why are you disquieted within me?" (Ps. 42:5). We can get the gist of the anthropologist's report that certain aboriginal cultures speak of a sickness called "soul loss." And no one of us fails to understand the words of an elderly, feeble woman admitted to the Burghölzli psychiatric clinic in Zurich. She had told her doctors she was dead and had lost her heart. But when the psychiatrist asked her to place her hand over her breast to feel her heart beating—"It must still be there if you can feel it beating" —she responded, "That is not my real heart."[4]

Though we would be hard pressed for a precise definition of what "soul" is, none of us can deny the sense of an inner reality, something more than vein, muscle, and tissue, constituting the heart of who we are as persons who leap at hope, are bowed at despair, who pray and plan, love and mourn, are stirred up by gross injustice, and who engage in an ongoing pilgrimage, to mention only a few of its dimensions. Though its immortal character (a continuing suspicion and an article of faith) cannot be demonstrated, its reality can hardly be denied. The Greeks gave it the name *psyche;* English-speaking persons substituted a derivative from the Old English *sāwl.* The Romans preferred the term *anima,* the Hebrews *nephesh,* and the French *âme.* While the great disparity of etymological roots is no doubt attributable to the ineffability of the subject, no language seems to wish to be found without some term to signify this reality and to talk about its ways.

The Reality of the Soul in Jung's Thought

In the opening chapter of *Religion and the Cure of Souls in Jung's Psychology,* Hans Schaer writes:

> Jung's psychology does not say: man has a soul or psyche. It says rather: man, as a psycho-physical being, partakes of psychic reality, or even, he is a part of psychic reality. The moment you start on Jung's psychology you have the feeling of entering into a spacious

new world that contains wide tracts of unknown territory and many secrets, and that accordingly holds out all sorts of possibilities of discovery. This new world is the world of the soul or the psyche, these terms being understood in their broadest sense. Just as the physical world known to us in modern science—in physics and chemistry on the one hand and astronomy on the other—extends into the infinitely great and the infinitesimally small without our having been able as yet to reach the limits of physical reality, so Jung presents the world of the psychic as infinite in extension.[5]

Describing his own work, Jung writes:

> The reality of the soul is the hypothesis with which I work and my main activity consists in collecting factual material and describing and explaining it. I have neither worked out a system nor a general theory but only postulated concepts which serve as tools, as is usual in any science.[6]

Many of Jung's colleagues, of course, issued disclaimers. Some denied the reality of the psyche/soul out of hand, restricting their definition of the real to things material and concrete. Others preferred to relegate the psyche/soul to a secondary order of reality, identifying it as an epiphenomenon of the nervous system or the brain.

Jung repudiated both camps. Though he could accept the soul's contiguity with the physical, he could not accept the analysis of soul as nothing but the physical.

> A psychology that treats the psyche as an epiphenomenon, would better call itself brain-psychology, and remain satisfied with the meagre results that such a psycho-physiology can yield. The psyche deserves to be taken as a phenomenon in its own right; there are no grounds for regarding it as an epiphenomenon, dependent though it may be on the functioning of the brain. One would be as little justified in regarding life as an epiphenomenon of the chemistry of carbon compounds.[7]

To reduce soul to a brain function would be comparable to reducing a Bach mass to a physiological process, a Monet oil to a chemical process, or a rose petal to an electromagnetic field. Though dependent on physical nature, the psyche/soul has a nature of its own, manifesting an impressive autonomy and independence that carries the physical body in the wake of its schemes and plans, rather than the reverse.

The exploration of the psyche/soul has developed along two lines.

One, as employed by most psychoanalytic traditions (especially in the Freudian mode), comes at the psyche/soul from the back door, as it were, or from what Jung calls "the most repulsive end, that is to say with all these things which we do not wish to see."[8] From this perspective the psyche (the word *soul* is rarely used in this tradition) is approached as a piece of the world that needs fixing. Its dimensions are seen largely as the function of repressions, complexes, and neuroses from which one needs deliverance.

A second approach to the psyche/soul, adopted by Jungian analytical psychology and shared by most religious traditions, is to come through, if you will, the front door, though hardly ignoring the existence of other venues in the psyche. This approach regards the soul as the quintessence of the self, the inner person, a center of creativity, value judgment-making, goal-setting, the foundry of dreams and intuitions, and the source of metaphysical speculation and religious feeling, the latter of which was of special interest to Jung.

> The soul possesses by nature a religious function. . . . But were it not a fact of experience that supreme values reside in the soul . . . psychology would not interest me in the least, for the soul would then be nothing but miserable vapor. I know, however, from hundredfold experience that it is nothing of the sort, but on the contrary contains the equivalents of everything that has been formulated in dogma and a good deal more. . . . I did not attribute religious functions to the soul. I merely produced the facts which prove that the soul is *naturaliter religiosa,* i.e., possesses a religious function.[9]

For Jung, the psyche/soul is "part of the inmost mystery of life," an "unimaginable complexity" at which Jung says "I can only gaze with wonder and awe."[10] Oddly, Jung observes, "The individual imagines that he has caught the psyche and holds her in the hollow of his hand. He is even making a science of her. . . . In reality the psyche is the mother and the maker, the subject and even the possibility of consciousness itself." In the end we may be far less the masters than the servants of our psyche/souls that reach "so far beyond the boundaries of consciousness that the latter could be easily compared to an island in the ocean."[11] "Our psyche, which is primarily responsible for all the historical changes wrought by the hand of man on the face of this planet, remains an insoluble puzzle and an incomprehensible wonder, an object of abiding perplexity—a feature it shares with all Nature's secrets."[12]

Psyche/Soul in the New Testament

For readers of Scripture, it is noteworthy that the New Testament concurs with Jung at most points on the nature and significance of the psyche/soul. Though the reader of the English New Testament may not always realize it, the word *soul* is a translation term for the Greek word *psyche* which occurs 102 times in the New Testament. The New Testament writers did not invent the term; they borrowed it from the hellenistic world where it enjoyed broad usage as a term to denote the "life principle" that enlivens the body during one's lifetime and departs at death. It is the center of emotions, longings, intentions, both spiritual and physical, constituting that spiritual-emotional-mental complex that more than any other ingredient identifies an individual's special personality and uniqueness and demonstrates the distinctive qualities of humanness. It is little wonder that Freud, when casting about for an appropriate term to describe the phenomenon he was observing on the couch, turned to *psyche* to convey his meaning.

What is the psyche/soul in the New Testament? It embraces a complex of related meanings. It can refer to "life" or the "life principle," as seen in Matthew 2:20 where King Herod seeks the *psyche* of the infant Jesus, translated "life." It can also denote the feeling, emotional, valuing center of the self, as in Luke 1:46, where we hear the words of the young Mary, "My *psyche* magnifies the Lord," or in Mark 12:30, where we hear the words of Jesus to his disciples to love the Lord with their whole *psyches,* translated "soul." The *psyche* can be stirred up (Acts 14:2), unsettled (Acts 15:24), subjected to temptation (2 Pet. 2:14), and besieged by the passions (1 Pet. 2:11).

From the New Testament standpoint, no matter how the psyche/soul is spoken of it is still regarded as the most precious of human endowments. We are told not to fear those who can destroy our bodies but not our *psyches,* but to fear him who can destroy both body and *psyche* (Matt. 10:28). We are told that to gain the whole world and lose our *psyches* constitutes an incomparable and unreclaimable loss (Mark 8:36). The most important item on the human agenda in New Testament perspective is the life of the psyche/soul, its preservation

(Heb. 10:39), its firm anchoring (Heb. 6:19), its purification (1 Pet. 1:22), and its securing (1 Pet. 1:9; James 1:21), a task to which the church, as keepers of our *psyches* (Heb. 13:17), and Christ, as "shepherd and guardian" of our *psyches* (1 Pet. 2:25) are committed.

How does one secure one's psyche/soul? One of the most striking paradoxes in the New Testament is that the psyche/soul cannot save itself. In fact, we are told, the more the psyche/soul is bent on winning itself, the more it is apt to lose (Mark 8:35). Following the model of the Son of man who offers his *psyche* as ransom for others (Mark 10:45), we learn that the highest calling of the *psyche* is to lay itself down for its friends (John 15:13), to risk itself for others (Acts 15:56; 20:24; Phil. 2:30; Rom. 16:4; 2 Cor. 12:15). In its most hyperbolic form this paradox is expressed by the shocking enjoinder that unless one "hates" his own *psyche* he cannot become a follower (Luke 14: 26).

Enlisting one's psyche/soul in service to others is the only way to allow for the growth of the psyche/soul. It derives its food and nourishment not from filled barns and sated appetites (Luke 12:20), but from the power of the "implanted word" (James 1:21). In the end its salvation and security depends on the individual's capacity to give oneself away for the good news (Mark 8:35), submitting its will to the divine will and entrusting its future to a "faithful creator" (1 Pet. 4:19).

In the New Testament, the term *psyche* comes closer than any other term to capturing the essence of what Jung intends with the world *Self.* Not the prideful, defensive, designing, ego-self, bent on its own safety, but rather a deeper, broader self that knows of its mortality, acknowledges its need for wholeness, and recognizes in a glass darkly that it participates in a meaning that transcends its present body, time, and place. The ultimate peril is not death nor suffering, but the misunderstanding and—at worst—the loss of *psyche.* For the New Testament as for Jung, the psyche/soul is real, and its nature and destiny remain the controlling issue and dominant life problem.

Scripture as the Utterance of Soul: Answer to Job

In 1952, Jung undertook an essay called *Answer to Job,* published first in German and four years later in English by the Pastoral Psychology Book Club in the United States. Jung wrote hesitantly, knowing the storm he might unleash with a book that touched on a psychological understanding of Scripture. Yet he felt impelled to write because of the questions raised by his earlier volume, *Aion,* published in 1951, dealing with the nature of the Christ symbol and the psychology of Christianity, and because of continual "questions from the public and from patients" that made Jung feel he must express himself "more clearly about the religious problems of modern man."[13]

Contrary to the suggestion of the title, the 130-page essay does not limit itself to a discussion of Job. It ranges widely, from Ezekiel to the Apocalypse, from John to Paul, from the Wisdom literature to the Johannine epistles, and devotes an unexpected amount of space to the 1950 Papal Dogma on the Assumption of Mary and the meaning such a dogma might signify in the mid-twentieth century.

Jung's posture in the book, as we noted earlier, is not that of a biblical scholar, "which I am not," Jung writes, but that of a "layman and physician who has been privileged to see deeply into the psychic life of many people."[14] His purpose is to come to a clearer understanding of the meaning of religious statements, whether in Scripture or in creeds and dogmas, not with respect to the physical facts they report but with respect to the psychic facts they demonstrate and convey as "testimonies of the soul."

A statement that sets forth Jung's thesis as clearly as any is found in the prologue:

> . . . Religious statements are psychic confessions, which in the last resort are based on unconscious, i.e., on transcendental, processes. These processes are not accessible to physical perception but demonstrate their existence through the confessions of the psyche. The resultant statements are filtered through the medium of human consciousness: that is to say, they are given visible forms. . . . Whenever we speak of religious contents we move in a world of images that point to something ineffable. We do not know how clear or unclear these images, metaphors, and concepts are in respect of their transcendental object. . . . I am also too well aware of how limited are our powers of conception. . . . But, although our whole world of religious ideas consists of anthropomorphic images that could never stand up to rational criticism, we should never forget that they are based on numinous archetypes, i.e., on . . . [a] foundation which is unassailable by reason. We are dealing with psychic facts which logic can overlook

but not eliminate. In this connection Tertullian has already appealed, quite rightly, to the testimony of the soul. In his *De testimonio animae,* he says:

> These testimonies of the soul are as simple as they are true
> . . . as divine as they are natural. I think that they cannot appear
> to any one to be trifling and ridiculous if he considers the maj-
> esty of Nature, whence the authority of the soul is derived.
> . . . Nature is the mistress, the soul is the disciple; what the one
> has taught, or the other has learned, has been delivered to them
> by God, who is, in truth, the Master even of the mistress herself.
> What notion the soul is able to conceive of her first teacher is
> in your power to judge, from that soul which is in you. Feel that
> which causes you to feel; think upon that which is in forebodings
> your prophet. . . . Strange if, being given by God, she knows how
> to act the diviner for men! Equally strange if she knows Him by
> whom she has been given!

I would go a step further and say that the statements made in the Holy Scriptures are also utterances of the soul. . . .[15]

Though it is not possible here to deal with all the psychological, theological, historical, and hermeneutical issues intimated in this ex-tended quotation and addressed in *Answer to Job* as a whole, it may be well to identify four key propositions that inform Jung's thesis about Scripture and constitute central concepts in his thinking about religious statements in general.

First, *all religious statements are rooted in the psyche/soul.* One of Jung's central theses is that not only all religious statements, but all human artifacts, whether in stone or wood, sound or form, act or speech, are products of the psyche/soul. They are not always rational and benign from the standpoint of consciousness, nor are they neces-sarily the result of conscious intention. But they are all the products of the states, insights, and propensities of the psyche/soul. Every stone sculpture and gum wrapper, every skyscraper and country gar-den, every religious custom and family tradition—as well as hospitals and churches, political parties and social programs, art, economics, military strategy, even psychology—is the record of the movements of the psyche/soul, bringing its mysteries and intentions to bear on the ordering and shaping of a world. One can say that the history of human culture is at the same time the history of the human soul, and, as a corollary, that the history of religious statements shares that process.

Second, *a religious statement is a psychic fact.* Jung is continually amazed at the modern rationalist temperament with its "strange supposition that a thing is true only if it presents itself as a *physical* fact."[16] There are not only physical facts, Jung contends; there are also psychic facts.

What is a psychic fact? Anything produced in the psyche experienced by the self: a dream, a fear, a vision of the future, a burning resentment, a hypothesis the mind arrives at, a hope seeded in the heart, a conviction that draws one's allegiance, a love that knows no discouragement. Not physical but psychic, and as real and palpable in personal biography and social history as any building or battle.

Religious statements fall in this category. Jung calls them "psychic confessions."[17] Spawned in the soul, they grow and gather weight until one day the right words and images are found to utter them publicly. Though couched in reasonable, rational forms, they are hardly the offspring of logic nor are they dependent on physical data, but are born of a light that is struck in the soul by a thought, word, or deed that for a moment gives a glimpse of a numinous reality beyond telling. Thus religious statements have to do with psychic truths rather than physical ones, and aim at illuming the life of the soul far more than providing physical data. If this were not the case, Jung states, they would "necessarily be treated in the textbooks of natural science. But religious statements without exception have to do with the reality of the *psyche* and not with the reality of *physis.*"[18]

To be sure, religious statements do traffic in physical facts. The Hebrew Scriptures speak of the "facts" of creation, of the call of Abraham, the Exodus, Exile, and building of the temple. The New Testament tells of the "facts" of the incarnation, crucifixion, resurrection, and day of Pentecost. Some of these would be classified by the scientific historian as clearly probable, others as physically improbable. Whether probable or not, Jung contends that when we examine the role these physical facts play in religious statements, we must consider whether it is the physical fact in itself that is being pro-

claimed, or the spiritual meaning that has gathered itself to this fact
as a form indigenous to its expression, that is being proclaimed. Is it
solely the "physical fact" of Jesus' crucifixion that Paul preaches, or
the "wisdom of the cross" he finds there; is it solely the "physical fact"
of Jesus' resurrection the gospels proclaim, or their experience of the
living Christ as God's designated Messiah and Lord of the Christian
community; is it solely the "physical fact" of the virgin birth that
Matthew and Luke proclaim, or the soulful conviction that Jesus is
a unique son of the Father, born not merely of the will of the flesh,
nor of the will of man, but of God? With respect to the Dogma of the
Assumption, Jung would ask, is it solely the "physical fact" of the
assumption of Mary to the realm of the Father that is being proclaimed, or, among other truths, a growing conscious awareness of the
"at-homeness" of the feminine in the realm of the divine?[19]

The time has come, in Jung's judgment, to shed the perspective
of the rationalist historian in evaluating the truth of religious statements in general and the statements of Scripture in particular. Truth
is larger than "physical fact." To regard "beliefs such as the virgin
birth, divine filiation, the resurrection of the dead, transubstantiation,
etc." as mere "moonshine,"[20] or to interpret a religious pronounce-
ment such as the Dogma of the Assumption as an intellectual "slap
in the face" (as the "rationalist historian" is apt to do), indicates a
mentality out of contact with the meaning to be found in metaphor,
symbol, and allegory, and a point-of-view that fails to recognize the
vernacular which the psyche/soul employs to convey its truth. Jung
found the appearance of the Dogma of the Assumption—as startling
as it was to a strictly historical and rationalistic mentality—to provide
"a favorable opportunity" for the biblical interpreter "to ask himself
. . . what is the meaning not only of the new dogma but of all more
or less dogmatic assertions over and above their literal concretism"
and to "bend to the great task of reinterpreting all the Christian
traditions" which involve "a question of truths which are anchored
deep in the soul."[21]

Third, *the function of religious statements is the tutelage of souls,*
through the compensation of the conscious attitude of individuals as
well as of entire cultures and epochs. The purpose of religious statements is soul-making. It is not scientific instruction. Nor is it histori-

cal information. Rather it is the tutelage of the self on its origin and destiny, its essence and obligation.

From a psychological perspective, Jung describes this process as the "compensation" of one's conscious attitude by truths and insights that emerge, as it were, spontaneously and autonomously from the unconscious. The point can best be illustrated by referring to Jung's discussion of the role of great art and literature in the psychic life of a culture. He describes such visionary art as a kind of "public dreaming," functioning in the life of an entire culture in the same way dreams function in the life of an individual.

In some instances Jung sees the function of art as bringing to consciousness the unexpressed *desires* of an age:

> An epoch is like an individual; it has its own limitations of conscious outlook, and therefore requires a compensatory adjustment. This is effected by the collective unconscious in that a poet, a seer or a leader allows himself to be guided by the unexpressed desire of his times and shows the way, by word or deed, to the attainment of that which everyone blindly craves and expects—whether this attainment results in good or evil, the healing of an epoch or its destruction.[22]

In other instances Jung sees art's function as raising to consciousness the unarticulated *needs* of an age. He notes that "visionary literature" can "bring a one-sided, abnormal or dangerous state of consciousness into equilibrium in an apparently purposive way. . . . Recoiling from the unsatisfying present the yearning of the artist reaches out to that primordial image in the unconscious which is best fitted to *compensate* the insufficiency and one-sidedness of the spirit of the age. The artist seizes this image and in the work of raising it from the deepest unconsciousness he brings it into relation with conscious values, thereby transforming its shape, until it can be accepted by his contemporaries according to their powers."[23]

Long stretches of Jewish and Christian history demonstrate an analogous compensatory function of religious and scriptural statements in the consciousness of the Hebrew and Christian communities. From a psychological perspective, the truths to which such statements refer sometimes appear to ferment for centuries below the surface of consciousness, giving off occasional seismic signals in prophetic utterances here and there and waiting until the time is ripe to break into consciousness. In such times old revelations and sensibilities are replaced by the new; ancient covenants are superseded by modern ones; and yesterday's hopes and dreams are fulfilled in a surprising figure or word that speaks for the culture at large and even beyond.[24]

"All scripture," according to the author of 2 Timothy, "is inspired by God and profitable for teaching, for reproof, for correction, and for training in righteousness, that the man of God may be complete, equipped for every good work" (2 Tim. 3:16). Its function is to instruct the soul or, in psychological terms, to "compensate conscious attitudes" with a transcendent word. From Jung's standpoint the process continues, with Scripture holding within its depths, words and visions dimly heard but sorely needed, waiting to be brought to consciousness by souls alive to its truth and equal to the task of making it plain.[25]

Fourth, *religious statements are rooted in the experience of the transcendent.* We noted earlier Jung's statement in the prologue to *Answer to Job* that "religious statements are psychic confessions, which in the last resort are based on unconscious, i.e., on transcendental, processes." On the basis of his experience with dreams, which enter the field of consciousness unannounced and uninvited, and on the basis of the reports of poets, painters, and musicians who have been suddenly but inexplicably "inspired" with a new work, Jung does not find it strange to read of the biblical authors who speak of having been seized by the Word or Spirit of God with a vision, a command, or commission they cannot resist. David in 2 Samuel 23:2 reports: "The spirit of the LORD speaks by me, his word is upon my tongue." Jeremiah 1:9 tells of the Lord putting forth his hand and touching Jeremiah's mouth. The author of the Apocalypse recalls the voice he heard from heaven telling him to write (Rev. 14:13). Jesus adjures his disciples, "When they deliver you up, do not be anxious how you are to speak or what you are to say; for what you are to say will be given to you in that hour; for it is not you who speak, but the Spirit of your Father speaking through you" (Matt. 10:19).

The assumption throughout Scripture is that it is possible to be seized by a "word" that extends beyond one's conscious knowledge or intention. It is described in various ways: as the "Word of the Lord," "the breath of the Almighty," a "voice from heaven," or most commonly as the "spirit of God" or the "Holy Spirit." Paul attempts to describe the experience in 1 Corinthians 2:10–13:

> For the Spirit searches everything, even the depths of God. For what person knows man's thought except the spirit of the man which is in him? So also no one comprehends the thoughts of God except the Spirit of God. Now we have received not the spirit of the world, but the Spirit which is from God, that we might understand the gifts bestowed on us by God. And we impart this in words not taught by human wisdom but taught by the Spirit, interpreting spiritual truths to those who possess the Spirit.

In Jung's understanding, such phenomena are analogous to dreams and waking visions which assault consciousness with a spontaneity and autonomy that one finds difficult to resist and impossible to take conscious credit for:

> Ideas of this kind are never invented, but enter the field of inner perception as finished products, for instance in dreams. They are spontaneous phenomena which are not subject to our will, and we are therefore justified in ascribing to them a certain autonomy. They are to be regarded not only as objects but as subjects with laws of their own. From the point of view of consciousness, we can, of course, describe them as objects, and even explain them up to a point, in the same measure as we can describe and explain a living human being. But then we have to disregard their autonomy. If that is considered, we are compelled to treat them as subjects; in other words, we have to admit that they possess spontaneity and purposiveness, or a kind of consciousness and free will. . . . The tremendous effectiveness (mana) of these images is such that they not only give one the feeling of pointing to the *Ens realissimum,* but make one convinced that they actually express it and establish it as a fact.[26]

For Jung the psyche/soul is the place where the divine and the human intersect. Traditional theology and popular religious opinion have tended to think of the divine or the transcendent largely in terms of a transcendence "without." God is conceived as addressing humans from a mountaintop, a cloud, or through an angel from "above." Jung's understanding of the divine and the transcendent, however, suggests we might think also in terms of a transcendence "within," and of God as touching and leading the human soul from within. Standing with the author of the fourth gospel who speaks of the indwelling paraclete, with Paul who speaks of the Christian as God's temple in whom God's spirit dwells, and with the thirteenth-century Dominican mystic, Meister Eckhardt, who holds that "God alone in his Godhead is not in a state of bliss, but must be born in the human soul,"[27] Jung affirms, "It would be blasphemy to assert that God can manifest Himself everywhere save only in the human soul."[28]

Jung acknowledges that "we do not know how clear or unclear" our theological "images, metaphors, and concepts are in respect of their transcendental objects,"[29] and he is thoroughly conscious of the limitation of "our powers of conception—to say nothing of the feebleness and poverty of language."[30] But he insists, we are nevertheless "dealing with psychic facts," which logic cannot verify, but experience cannot deny, and it is to such transcendent "facts" and experiences to which Scripture attests.

Scripture: An Anthology of Soul

At the center of all scriptural expression is the consciousness of the numinous. Transparent to every word of Scripture is the One known as both revealed and hidden. The scriptural authors strain with all their art and within the limitations of their language and times to bring a faithful report of what they have heard and seen of this One.

The psyche/soul can voice its experience of the "holy" in many ways, not all of which are literary. Its virtuousity seems endless. It can build a sanctuary, construct an altar, design a healing sand painting, construct a creed, perform a deed of mercy, sketch a picture, mold an image, choreograph a dance, don a sacred vestment, design a stained glass mosaic, or perform a rite—as the traditions of Judaism and Christianity among others have demonstrated for generations. But it can also give voice to its knowledge in spoken and written word—in myth and love song, in legend and history, in psalm and proverb, prophetic dream and cultic law, in letters and creedal formulae, in hymns and doxologies, in prayers and religious tales, dirges and dramas, apocalypses and gospels.

The modes in which Scripture speaks betray the vast panoply of styles, talents, and perspectives of the scriptural authors. In Jungian terms, it is a literary "conjunction of opposites," containing within its covers orthodoxy and heterodoxy, universalism and parochialism, legalism and anti-nomianism, priestly traditionalism and prophetic moralism, this-worldly perspectives along with the other-worldly.

We also find hints of Jung's psychological types among the biblical authors. Some are highly *extroverted,* such as the writers of Genesis, Ruth, Jonah, and Luke-Acts, all of whom reach out to the world with their teachings and proclamations. Others appear to be more *introverted,* like Jeremiah, Ezra, or the author of the Apocalypse, who retreat from a world they find corrupted and corrupting. We find *feeling types,* speaking in moral indignation, like Matthew; *sensing types,* extolling physical love, like the Song of Songs; *thinking types,* attempting to plumb the mysteries of the wise man and the fool, like Proverbs; and *intuitive types,* who sense the eternal word in all things, like the Gospel according to John.

When one reads any of Scripture, one hears clearly the voices of the scriptural authors, speaking in their own tongues and cadences, their own vocabulary and syntax. But one also senses the overtones of the original voice and word they have heard. To continue with the biblical authors, is to allow ourselves to be drawn by their art into the presence of the One whose word and will echoes in their speech.

CHAPTER IV

Biblical Symbols:
The Vocabulary of the Soul

> Because there are innumerable things beyond the range of human
> understanding, we constantly use symbolic terms to represent con-
> cepts that we cannot define or fully comprehend. This is one reason
> why all religions employ symbolic language or images.
> —*Man and His Symbols*[1]

In a letter to a friend in Basel in 1952, Jung includes the following
personal note: "Recently an elderly Swiss clergyman wrote me a
touching letter emphasizing that through my writings I had *at last
opened the way to the Bible for him.* I certainly never expected that."
Jung adds, "But you can see from this that the figurative language of
the Bible is not understood even by a clergyman." With this statement
Jung is affirming the fundamental conviction that the language of the
Bible is inescapably drawn to the figurative and symbolic, and to come
to an appreciation of that fact is to open the way to a proper understanding of the meaning and purpose of Scripture.

The statement must be seen against Jung's background; certainly
Jung did not believe that all clergy, certainly not contemporary clergy,
fail to understand the figurative dimension of biblical language. But
Jung had found it strange that his father and uncles, all pastors whom
he dearly loved, seemed to treat the Bible as a book of historical facts,
as a book of scientific facts or as a book of theological facts rather than
as a book of life. He had thought it odd that they taught the Bible as

a book of information to be believed and mastered rather than as a book of transformation to be assimilated into one's bones.

The contrast is reflected in a story related by the great preacher Halford Luccock. The story, taken from Lloyd Lewis' life of General Sherman, tells of a teamster on the Union side in the Battle of Shiloh who was struggling to push a gunsling up the side of a muddy river bank when an evangelist from the Christian and Sanitary Commission came by with Bible in hand. He asked the teamster, "Do you know who died on a cross?" Without looking up, the man answered, "Don't ask me any riddles. I'm stuck in the mud."[2]

From Jung's perspective, the Bible as a soul book deals with issues that cannot be reduced to simple formulas, or slogans, or on-the-run question-and-answer catechesis. Its truths cannot be taken as a quick vaccination, once and for all. The issues Scripture deals with are far less manageable.

Of what issues does Scripture speak? It speaks of the meaning of our life and the meaning of our death, and of the mysteries of evil and suffering, as well as the mysteries of love and healing. It deals with the psychic fact of sin and guilt and the liberation that comes with forgiveness. It deals with the holy. Scripture deals with things beyond words, beyond simple formulation; at best they can be hinted at. And because it speaks of such realities, it is driven, as Jung would observe, to speak in stories, figures, and symbols.

What Is a Symbol?

In *Man and His Symbols* Jung states, "Because there are innumerable things beyond the range of human understanding, we constantly use symbolic terms to represent concepts that we can't define or fully comprehend. This is one reason why all religions employ symbolic language or images."[3] The Scripture writers understood this. Paul certainly knew about the limits of human knowledge and language. So did Isaiah and the fourth evangelist. They spoke of what they knew, but they admitted to partial vision. As an old German hymn reminds us, "See the moon in yonder sky; 'tis only half that meets the eye." Symbols deal with realities partially understood but also partially hidden from human understanding.

The etymology of the word *symbol* in fact suggests this. The word derives from two Greek roots, the prefix *sym,* which means "to-gether," and the verb *ballein* (whence the English word *ballistics*) which means "to throw." Thus a symbol "throws" two things "to-gether," a subject and the image that seems best equipped to capture its meaning. As Jung puts it, symbols provide us with images that are the "best possible formulation of a relatively unknown thing which cannot for that reason be more clearly or characteristically repre-sented."[4]

What are symbols for? Jung would answer, for soul-making, for awakening, cultivating, stimulating, deepening perception and growth in mind, heart, and will. In fact, Jesus of Nazareth used symbols that way. When asked a question he seldom gave a direct answer. Instead he would strike an image or tell a story to get his hearers to think rather than imitate. C. H. Dodd's classic definition of parable captures this symbol function of Jesus' teaching so well: "The parable is a metaphor or simile drawn from nature or common life, arresting the hearer by its vividness or strangeness, and leaving the mind in suffi-cient doubt about its precise application to tease it into active thought."[5]

From Jung's standpoint, symbols are the natural language of the soul. We produce symbols spontaneously in our dreams. We produce images and symbols in our everyday speech. From our private doo-dling to our public art, whether in business advertisements, in scien-tific journals, in religion and the arts, symbols surface to say what logic and plain speech cannot convey, at least not economically. Fur-thermore, Jung would say, all of us respond natively to symbols and we all know intuitively how to catch their meaning.

The writers of Scripture knew all this, or most of it. The Psalmist, the writers of proverbs, the tellers of tales and parables, the writers of apocalypse, all understood that meaning exceeds language, and that image, figure, story, and symbol can often succeed, where plain speech fails, in speaking to the whole person of the wholeness of the reality of which they would speak.

A Glossary of Biblical Symbols in Jungian Perspective

The power a living symbol has to evoke the deepest feelings, longings, and insights resides in the fact that it has the capacity to gain a hearing from more than just the rational and conscious side of the self. Jung observes that the symbol

> certainly has one side that accords with reason, but it has also another side that is inaccessible to reason. . . . The prospective meaning and pregnant significance of the symbol appeals just as strongly to thinking as to feeling, while its peculiar plastic imagery when shaped into sensuous form stimulates sensation as much as intuition.[6]

One sees this multi-faceted appeal at work in the symbols of Scripture. Though we cannot here explore individual biblical symbols in depth nor provide an exhaustive listing, we can indicate, on the basis of Jung's insight into the nature of symbols, some of the polyvalent ways in which symbols in general, and biblical symbols in particular, attract the soul's attention to the meanings they would convey, a process that draws on unconscious as well as conscious factors and appeals to the feeling as well as the thinking side of the self, the sensing as well as the intuitive.

Geometric Symbols. Although geometric symbols appear in the Bible only by allusion (the cross,[7] the circle,[8] and the square[9]), they do play an important role in the iconography of traditions that develop out of Scripture and, for our present purpose, illustrate with special effectiveness the unconscious factors at work in the origination and interpretation of symbols.

I have posed the question to study groups on occasion, whether a vertical line or a horizontal line would be the better image to symbolize the "heavenly" as opposed to the "earthly." Invariably the group points to the vertical. Likewise, when they are asked whether triangle A or triangle B would serve better to symbolize the "transcendent" as opposed to the "human," they invariably opt for the former. The reasons for the choice would seem fairly obvious, but the fact that the choice occurs so spontaneously and unanimously always comes as a surprise, especially when one follows up this exercise with questions about the meanings the group attaches to certain numbers or colors. The implication of the exercise is that, either due to cultural conditioning or to a native bent in the human psyche, our present

A

B

consciousness finds "vertical" and "upward-thrusting" images more expressive of transcendence than "horizontal" or "downward-thrusting" image, so that without any prior conscious training one can sense the connotations of a given symbol without consciously articulating what that connotation is.

To carry the exercise a bit further, when we combine a vertical with a horizontal we get the figure of a cross. When we combine the upward-thrusting triangle with the downward thrusting triangle, we come up with this image classically known as the Star of David or Solomon's Seal. As *signs,* the cross and the Star of David denote Christianity and Judaism respectively, but as *symbols* their geometric qualities in themselves are capable in our cultural milieu of mediating the notion, fundamentally "hidden" to consciousness, of the merging of the "divine" and "human," the "heavenly" and the "earthly."

Symbols carry with them not only denotative associations noted by consciousness but connotations registered primarily at the level of the unconscious, a fact that helps explain the arational but perduring power that a given symbol may exert over long periods of time.

Numerical Symbols. "The role that numbers play in mythology and in the unconscious," Jung comments, "gives food for thought."[10] In Scripture, numbers function both as *sign* and *symbol.* As *sign* a number most often will be a cryptogram for the name of someone or something. Both in ancient Hebrew and Greek, numbers were represented by the letters of the alphabet (e.g., A = 1, B = 2, C = 3), every word or name had a numerical value, and correlatively, any number could represent a word or name whose letter-values totalled up to that number. The classic example is the "beast" in Revelation 13:18 "whose number is 666," most likely referring either to Nero (NERON CAESAR in Hebrew letters = 666) or the Roman Empire (LATEINOS in Greek letters = 666).

As *symbol,* however, a number does not function as a code letter but as an image that connotes a quality, concept, or value that for reasons not entirely clear to consciousness have become associated with that number. Though it is not possible to draw up a precise dictionary of numerical symbols, it is possible to set forth some concepts that certain numbers in the ancient Near Eastern world and in Scripture have been found eminently well-suited to convey, again for reasons dimly apparent to reason.

When, for example, a group is asked to select a number that might best serve to symbolize God, they invariably come up with the number "one" (or "three" in Christian circles), with perhaps an added zero or two, e.g., 10, 100, 1000, signifying magnitude.

Three (3) is a number also commonly associated with the Godhead, in some instances connoting the notion of *generative unity and diversity* (two elements producing a third; mother, father, child; Father, Spirit, Son; Moses, Elijah, Jesus[11]). It is also associated with the idea of process (beginning, middle, end; past, present, future).

Four (4) is a symbolic number employed almost universally to express *realized wholeness or completeness.* One thinks of the four corners of the earth (Isa. 11:12; Rev. 7:1); the four cardinal points on the compass (Luke 13:29); the four Platonic virtues (wisdom, temperance, justice, and courage), along with the imagery of completeness suggested in the symbol of Israel wandering for 40 years in the wilderness or the 40 days of fasting by Moses (Exod. 34:28), Elijah (1 Kings 19:8), and Jesus (Mark 1:13).

Seven (7) and its multiple, 70, is one of the most widely used numbers in classical antiquity denoting *perfection.* Philo Judaeus, an Alexandrian Jewish philosopher contemporary with Jesus and Paul, devotes columns of his essay, *On the Creation of the World,* to the virtues of this "august" number. Scripture begins with the seven days of creation. The New Testament, especially the Jewish Christian tradition reflected in Matthew, James, and the book of Revelation, highlight this number: the seven petitions of the Lord's Prayer (Matt. 6:9–13), the seven parables of Matthew 13, the seven woes in Matthew 23, the seven gifts of heavenly wisdom in James 3:17, and the virtually endless series of sevens—seven churches, seven angels, seven trumpets, seven bowls of wrath, etc.—in Revelation. One recalls that the Feast of Pentecost or Feast of Weeks represents 7 × 7 days, plus 1 for good measure, beyond Passover in the Judaic tradition or Easter in the Christian.

It is most likely on the basis of ancient astronomy, which divided the solar year into twelve months, the heavens into twelve zodiacal zones, and day and night into twelve periods, that the number *twelve* becomes significant in Scripture: the twelve tribes, the twelve disciples, and the twelve gates of heaven (Rev. 21:12–14) as well as the 144 (= 12 × 12) souls sealed for salvation (Rev. 7:4). Itself the product of two highly respected numbers (3 × 4), a fact that does not escape comment by the ancients, twelve would seem to connote completeness of ultimate or cosmological importance.

In the fourth century, Augustine wrote that "the science of numbers is . . . of eminent service to the careful interpreter" of Holy Scripture and that "ignorance of numbers prevents us from understanding the things that are set down in Scripture in figurative and mystical ways."[12] Though we might not be as certain as Augustine of the specific value a biblical author might attach to a given number, we can take the words as a helpful enjoinder to become more sensitive to the symbolic value numbers might hold in the intention of the author as well as in the unconscious perceptions of the reader.

Color Symbolism. Jung noted early in his work on dream and art analysis that colors functioned symbolically and frequently added a significant and meaningful dimension to a drawing or dream:

> We have only to look at the drawings and paintings of patients . . . to see that colors are feeling-values. Mostly, to begin with, only a pencil or pen is used to make rapid sketches of dreams, sudden ideas, and fantasies. But from a certain moment . . . the patients begin to make use of colour . . . merely intellectual interest gives way to emotional participation. Occasionally the same phenomenon can be observed in dreams, which at such moments are dreamt in colour, or a particularly vivid colour is insisted upon."[13]

In Scripture as well, although there is no word for the concept of color itself, we find the symbolic use of color to convey thoughts, feelings, and concepts not at all surprising or improbable to the modern reader for whom these colors still have many of the same unconscious associations.[14]

The color *black,* predictably, connotes the dark side of human experience, mourning (Jer. 4:28), desolation (Isa. 50:3), treachery

(Job. 6:16), and cosmic judgment of evil (Rev. 6:12). *Blue* can connote wisdom (Ecclus. 6:30), but is also associated with the related hues of *purple* and *violet* which have broad associations with royalty. *Gray* connotes old age (Gen. 42:38) and *green,* flourishing health, vitality, luxuriance, and growth (Mark 6:39; Deut. 12:2). *Red* is etymologically related to the Hebrew word for "earth," but has obvious associations with blood and violence (Rev. 6:4). *White,* as expected, denotes purification (Ps. 51:7) and sanctity, as the color of the garments of angels (John 20:12), the risen Lord (Matt. 28:3) and those who will be saved (Rev. 7:9).

The point Jung would make about the symbolic significance of color in dreams, art, or Scripture is that it communicates values, feelings, and insights through a medium that speaks less to the rational, conscious mind than to the senses, feeling, and intuitions.

Symbolism of the Human Body. Though there is little if any explicit genital symbolism in Scripture, most every other part of the body is used in a symbolic way.

A key image to symbolize the divine will is the symbol of the *voice.* The young Samuel hears the voice of the Lord calling him in the sanctuary at Shiloh (1 Sam. 3:2ff.); the prophets also know this voice (e.g., Isa. 6:8; Jer. 3:13); it speaks at the baptism of Jesus (Mark 1:11) and the transfiguration (Mark 9:7); it thunders forth from the heavenly throne in Revelation (19:5); it addresses Peter in a dream (Acts 11:9) and Paul on the road to Damascus (Acts 9:4). It is spoken of ubiquitously in Rabbinic literature as the Bath Qol, the "heavenly voice," that can be heard even when God's presence may not be felt. In his Terry Lectures Jung reports the phenomenon of the voice as familiar both "in dreams and in other peculiar conditions of consciousness."[15]

Far more important than the *eye* in Hebrew Scriptures is the *ear* as a symbol. It does not denote the physical ear; one can fail to hear having ears (Jer. 5:21; Isa. 43:8). It speaks of an "inner ear" capable of hearing the voice of God and catching the Word.

Other images drawn from the human body include (a) the *nose,* often symbolizing anger (Exod. 15:8); (b) the *heart,* intellect (Prov. 14:33) and will (Prov. 16:9); (c) the *kidneys,* emotions (Prov. 23:16);

(d) the *bowels,* love and sympathy (Song of Songs 5:4); (e) the *liver,* the center of life (Prov. 7:23); (f) the *face,* symbolizing the presence and *persona* of the divine (Ps. 11:7; Exod. 33:14–15; Deut. 5:4f.); (g) *blood,* signifying the life principle itself and the bonding or covenant-ing that can take place between the divine and the human (Lev. 17:11; Deut. 12:23); (h) the symbols of *right* and *left,* reflecting the sense of duality in the human psyche, the *right* representing the light or fa-vored side (Job 40:1; Matt. 25:33) and the *left* the dark or disfavored side (Judg. 3:15; Matt. 25:33).[16]

Animal Symbolism. One has only to look at children's stories, fairy tales, TV cartoons, magazine ads, and the names of professional sports teams and automobile models to see the natural role animal symbolism assumes in the human psyche. The church in recent cen-turies has tended to eliminate animal imagery except in its most representative forms, e.g., Noah on his ark and the Good Shepherd leading his flock.

A reason for playing down animal symbolism may of course lie in its native fitness for symbolizing the instinctual side of the self, which includes the unleashed and destructive side of the self. But animal symbolism can also point to constructive instinctual powers. In Scripture we find both uses. The *bull, wolf, viper,* and *scorpion* are employed to symbolize the rampant sexuality, voracity, and poison-ous qualities potentiable in the human soul. In the apocalyptic litera-ture we find images of *supra-natural beasts* and *dragons* to depict in surrealistic magnitude the immense destructiveness of which human —not animal—nature is capable. But we also find the images of the *dove, lamb,* and *ant* to represent the spirituality, innocence, and shrewd industry possible in the human soul.

One of the most memorable constructive tableaux of animal sym-bolism is found in the vision of what Edward Hicks, the nineteenth-century American painter, called "The Peaceable Kingdom," the portrait of the wolf lying down with the lamb, the leopard with the kid, and the calf, lion, and fatling together (Isa. 11:6f.).[17]

Nature Symbolism. Because of their association with "paganism," the images of the sun, moon, stars, and planets are rarely used in Scrip-ture. Beyond this omission, the scriptural writers join with virtually every other religious tradition in using symbols drawn from nature to express the holy.

Among the images drawn from the land, one thinks of the *wilderness*, both in the Hebrew Scriptures and New Testament, symbolizing the wasteland through which the soul finds itself traveling, a time of testing but also ironically a time of new inner vision. One thinks of the image of the *mountain* as a symbol of theophany (Exod. 19—20; Matt. 5—7), of spiritual transfiguration (Mark 9:1–8), of heavenly ascent (Acts 1:12, cf. vss. 6–11), and of the dwelling place for the eternal temple (Isa. 2:2; Ezek. 40:2; Rev. 21:10). One thinks also of the *rock* and the *stone*, peerless symbols for that which withstands the eroding forces of time: God, the *rock* (Ps. 42:9), the house built on *rock* (Matt. 7:24), Peter the *rock* (Matt. 16:18), the two tablets of *stone* of the decalogue (Deut. 4:13), the *stones* of witness (Gen. 31:46), and Christ, the *rock* (1 Cor. 10:4). Jung comments: "The stone has no uncertainties . . . and is eternally the same for thousands of years . . . while I am only a passing phenomenon . . . like a flame that flares up quickly and then goes out."[18]

Turning to images drawn from "the elements" and "the sea," we find the *wind* as a natural image to express the powerful but invisible movements of the divine (Gen. 1:2; John 3:8; Acts 2:2) as seen in the fact that both in Hebrew *(ruach)* and Greek *(pneuma)* the word for "wind" is also the word for "spirit." The image of the *storm* is used to symbolize the powerful darkness that can be experienced, at the hand of God (Ps. 83:15; Nah. 1:3), at the hand of his prophets (Ezek. 38:9) or at the hand of evil men (Isa. 25:4). *Thunder* and *lightning* frequently symbolize divine illumination (Exod. 19:16; Matt. 24:27; Rev. 8:5). One of the most ubiquitous symbols is that of the *water*, the *sea*, and *the deep*, symbolizing variously (a) the primordial powers held at bay by the divine rebuke (Isa. 51:10; Exod. 14:21; Ps. 104:6–7; Mark 4:39); (b) the unordered matrix of all being (Gen. 1) as well as the mysterious depths in which life can be swallowed up (Jon. 1; Matt. 14:30; Mark 5:13); (c) the uterine waters of spiritual rebirth (John 3:5) and the "living water" that quenches the soul's thirst forever (John 4:10–14); and (d) in contemporary dream and art analysis, the depths of the unconscious where "deep calls to deep" (Ps. 42:7).

From agriculture (a) the *seed*, symbolizes the seminal power at work both in the spiritual and material worlds (Mark 4:31; Luke 8:5ff.; Gal. 3:29); (b) the *harvest,* symbolizes the natural process which, in God's own time, brings the most modest of efforts to astonishing fruition (Mark 4:26–29); and (c) the *tree* symbolizes the physical and spiritual growth rooted in the divine (Ps. 1:3; Prov. 11:30), a meaning retained even when in Christian tradition the tree is identified with the cross (1 Pet. 2:24).

Socio-Cultural Symbols from Everyday Life. We can cite only a few of the vast number of domestic, social, economic, and political images used symbolically in Scripture. They include *domestic* images, e.g., the *house,* found universally as a symbol of the self (Matt. 7:24f.); the *door,* symbolizing a route of access that needs only to be tried (Rev. 3:8, 20); the *key,* a transparent symbol for the solution to a problem or of the power to execute the divine will (Matt. 16:19; Rev. 1:18). We also find *kitchen symbols: salt* (Matt. 5:13) symbolizing the "worth" of the self; *bread* and *wine,* symbolizing the "true" nourishment of blood and body; the *cup,* symbolizing one's "lot" (Luke 22:14–23); and the *table,* adumbrating a final conjunction of opposites in which the sacred and profane (Mark 2:15; Matt. 22:10), the clean and the unclean (Matt. 14:21), and those from North and South, East and West (Luke 13:29) will be brought together.

From the *trades and professions* we encounter the image of the *fisher* as "searcher" and the *fish* as those who can be "caught" by the Word (Mark 1:16f.); the *shepherd* as pastor and the *sheep* as those in a pastor's care (Luke 12:32; John 10:11; Ezek. 34:11–31); the *physician,* formerly a healer of one's *physis* or physical nature, now a curer of souls (Mark 2:17; Jer. 8:22); the *vineyard* as God's planted people (Isa. 5:1–7; Jer. 12:10) and the *vine* as a symbol of the organic unity between the divine and the human (John 15:1–11).

Among images drawn from the *family unit,* we find the predominant image to be that of God as *father,* symbolizing divine procreation of all people and things (1 Cor. 8:6; Isa. 64:8; Mal. 2:10; Eph. 4:6), though there are instances of the symbolic use of *mother* (Mark 3:34f.), *sister* (Rom. 16:1, 15; 1 Cor. 7:15) and *brother* (Rom. 16:14; James 1:2). We also find instances of the image of the *wedding* or *marriage,* common in the dreaming, art, and literature of the world as a symbol of the conjunction of opposites and the creation of a new unity out of disjoined parts (Matt. 22:1–4; Luke 14:16–24; Rev. 19:7).

Other images include *athletic symbols* which compare the spiritual life to an athletic contest (2 Tim. 4:7; Heb. 12:1); *military symbolism* that speaks of spiritual armour for spiritual warfare (1 Thess. 5:8); symbolism from the *institution of slavery* that speaks of slavery to sin and the passions (Rom. 6:6; Titus 3:3) and of *redemption* from such bondage (Rom. 8:23); symbolism from the *political sphere* that tells of a realm in which God is king and of a "commonwealth of heaven" (Phil. 3:20) as well as of a community of spiritually enfranchised citizens *(ekklesia)* (1 Thess. 1:1, etc.). The *names of nations* also are used symbolically, no longer to refer to a geographic entity but a spiritual one, symbolizing "bondage" (Egypt, Hos. 11:5) or "wickedness" (Babylon-Rome, Rev. 17:5; 18:10). From the field of *economics and trade* we hear of the spiritual investment of one's "talents" (a biblical image that makes its way into English as a standard metaphor; Matt. 25:14–30), of the "interest" that accrues to such an investment (Phil. 4:17), and of the spiritual richness (e.g., 1 Tim. 6:18) or poverty (Luke 12:21) that characterizes life. Finally, from the *religious-cultic sphere* we hear of a spiritual high priest (Heb. 10:2) in a heavenly sanctuary (Heb. 8:5) having performed an eternal sacrifice (Heb. 9: 14), and of the soul as the *temple* of God (1 Cor. 3:16).

Personal Symbolism. One of the distinctive marks of biblical religion is the central role biblical personalities play. Individuals from the biblical past become representative figures for the present. *Adam* becomes the image of one's fallible humanity, somehow created for something more; *Abraham* inspires a promethean, venturesome faith; *Solomon* calls forth wisdom; *Ruth,* familial fidelity; *Dorcas,* compassion and generosity; *Peter* reminds us that we too may be called to be "rocks" in spite of ourselves; *Judas* mirrors our darkest side; *Mary Magdalene* speaks to us of the saved soul; *John the Baptist* dares us to be a "voice crying in the wilderness"; and *Paul* shows us a person "turned around" and enlisted by God. Add *Mary* and *Martha, Cain* and *Abel, Mary* and *Joseph, Jacob* and *Esau,* a boundless list—and one finds a cast of characters broad enough to reflect the spectrum of life experience.

Supra-natural Symbolism. A final class of symbols includes images that attempt to name the numinous itself. They include the symbols of "God" and "Satan," "heaven" and "hell," "angels" and the "powers of darkness." The fact that "no one has ever seen God" (John 1:18)[19] does not discourage the authors of Scripture from speaking of their experience of the divine and devising a broad vocabulary of divine names to symbolize the quality of the divine disclosed in religious experience. These *divine names* and symbols of the numinous include: (a) Father (Matt. 6:9), Maker of Heaven and Earth (Gen. 14:19), Fountain of Life (Ps. 36:9), and the Living God (Hos. 1:10) symbolizing the procreativity and care of the numinous; (b) the Holy One (Isa. 6:3), Exalted One (Gen. 14:18), and the Most High, symbolizing the "otherness" and "transcendence" of the divine; (c) God of the Mountain, God Almighty (Exod. 6:3), expressing divine power; (d) the Everlasting (Gen. 21:33), the Rock (Isa. 30:29), the Ancient of Days (Dan. 7:9), and the First and the Last (Isa. 44:6), symbolizing the eternality and timelessness of the divine; (e) the Judge (Gen. 18:25) expressing divine righteousness; (f) the King (Ps. 24) symbolizing God's dominion; (g) the God of your Fathers (Exod. 3:15), God of Abraham, Isaac, and Jacob (Exod. 3:15), the Mighty One of Jacob (Gen. 49:24), Redeemer (Isa. 41:14), Savior (Ps. 62:6), and God and Father of our Lord Jesus Christ (Eph. 1:3) symbolizing the sense of God's using the destiny and mission of a particular people and history to carry out the divine will. Most prominent of all the divine names is the personal name (h) transliterated as Yahweh or Jehovah (and translated as "Lord" in modern English translations). This above all other divine titles in Scripture makes plain the fundamental biblical assumption that no name is capable of capturing the nature and reality of the numinous and that all theological formulations are to some extent "words without knowledge" (Job 38:2) and the utterance of "what is not understood" (Job 42:2). Representing four Hebrew letters, the name *Yahweh* was not pronounced or spoken in early Judaism. This was not only to avoid the risk of taking the divine name in vain but also to symbolize ritually that the divine essence is ineffable and "holy," beyond human speaking and comprehension.

Turning to the imagery of *Satan* and the *demonic,* we find relatively few instances in Hebrew Scripture. It is only after 300 B.C. that we find a large number of images enlisted to capture the experience of the "one" called *Satan* in Hebrew and *Devil (diabolos)* in Greek, both terms meaning "the Obstructer." The other names by which this reality is symbolized include: "the evil one" (Matt. 13:19), "the tempter" (Matt. 4:3); "the plaintiff" (1 Pet. 5:8) or "accuser" (Rev. 12:10), "the enemy" (Matt. 13:39), the "prince of demons" (Matt. 9:34), the "ruler of this world" (John 12:31), the "prince of the power of the air" (Eph. 2:2), "the liar" and "father of lies" (John 8:44), and the "great dragon" and "ancient serpent" (Rev. 12:9). At times a proper name is used: Beliar or Belial (= "worthlessness"; 2 Cor. 6:15) and Beelzebul (= "Lord of the flies" or "Lord of Dung"; Matt. 10:25). Though the literature is not in agreement on his mythic origins —was he the rebel ringleader of the "sons of God" or the rebel angel Lucifer (Enoch 54:6; Slav. Enoch 39:4; 2 Cor. 11:14; Job 1:6–12; Isa. 14:12) ?—his identity is plain as the author of discord, deception, violence, moral ignorance and darkness, and even illness and death.

Why would anyone elaborate such imagery and develop such an extensive symbolism of evil? A probable clue is found in the response of a Boston psychiatrist to the question, "What do you think of the use of such terms as 'Satan' and 'devil'?" His response was, "On the basis of my experience in the psychiatric wards, I am often more inclined to believe in the reality of the devil than in the reality of God." It is out of an analogous experience that apocalyptic literature emerges, when the numinous power of darkness overshadows the light, when normal human beings allow their consciences to be darkened and perform monstrosities that numb the mind, in such times the symbolism of "heaven" vs. "hell," of "angels of light" vs. the "forces of darkness," of many-headed monstrous beasts and of Armageddons erupt from the unconscious as easily as the psalms praising the immeasurable goodness of God appear on the lips when life has been filled with unspeakable grace.

The world as the biblical writers see it is of supra-natural proportions, or to use the synonymous Greek root, *meta-physical,* "above the physical." It is not just a world of colors, numbers, animals, and trees, of farmers and merchants, as poignant and appealing as that might be. The "real world" in biblical perspective is the one that plays itself out *through* these things. It is a world in which the primary realities are "the good" and "the evil," the "life-giving" and the "life-depriving," the "just" and the "unjust," the "light" and the "darkness," the "saving" and the "destroying," the "holy" and the "unholy," the "godly" and the "demonic." To fail to talk about these realities because they are not so readily visible or because conventional language balks at the assignment is no excuse for silence. Utilizing the limits of language, the writers of Scripture break out into speech enlisting images and symbols to report what they have heard and seen to eyes that may not have seen, nor ears heard, nor the heart conceived.

Scripture, the Soul, and the Symbolic Life

In his autobiography Jung advocates what he calls the "symbolic life":

> I have frequently seen people become neurotic when they content themselves with inadequate or wrong answers to the questions of life. They seek position, marriage, reputation, outward success or money, and remain unhappy and neurotic even when they have attained what they were seeking. Such people are usually confined within too narrow a spiritual horizon. Their life has not sufficient content, sufficient meaning. . . .
> . . . the believer has the opportunity, in his church, to live the "symbolic life." We need only think of the experience of the Mass, of baptism, of the *imitatio Christi,* and many other aspects of religion. But to live and experience symbols presupposes a vital participation on the part of the believer, and only too often this is lacking in people today.[20]

The reasons for cultivating the "symbolic life" are manifold. In the first place, without symbols we are deaf, dumb, and blind to those realities that defy hearing, speaking, and seeing in a conventional sense. Without the right word or the right image, certain realities remain "closed to us."[21] Without an image to recall it, certain dimensions of our experience become lost. Without symbolism, in Goethe's words, we lack tools to transform "the phenomenon into idea and the idea into image"; for it is "in the image" that "the idea remains infinitely effective."[22]

Second, there is a moral dimension to the "symbolic life," for without symbols we are apt to lose sight of certain truths of our own being and of our culture. Where rational argument remains deadlocked and logic moot, the story, the figure, the allusion and image can shed the light that makes our acts and motives plain and opens up the possibility that we might actually see ourselves as we really are, as well as what we might be.

Third, we need symbols to catalyze our powers. Time and again we hear of the right word spoken at the right time. It was the image of the "field white for harvest" from John's gospel (4:35) that dispelled the confusion of a German friend who, after a mindless war, had lost his direction. When we find ourselves without hope, without a way, great and powerful symbols can emerge to catalyze our energies and enlist our powers so that we are "renewed like eagles."

Scripture and religious tradition in general are repositories of such symbols. Jung states that the Roman Catholic Church has provided "the greatest objectification of . . . symbols the West has ever known,"[23] charting a galactic glossary of all the stages of the soul. Scripture provides much the same thing, though Protestant tradition has not been sufficiently conscious of that fact.

The language of symbol in Scripture has meanings that are fluid and depths that exceed the reach of natural vision. Images that on the surface are homely and prosaic are held up to the light to disclose deeper truths. Beginning with the known, the scriptural symbol invites contemplation of the unknown. Using the familiar as a touchstone, it leads the reader to consideration of the unfamiliar. Commencing with facts and probabilities known to the conscious mind, it gestures toward possibilities intuited by the soul. It does not blanch at evil nor does it overestimate the good in humankind, but it does draw attention to the broader story of which both are part. When we deal with scriptural language we are not dealing in univocal, unambiguous "signs" aimed at economy of meaning, but with polyvalent images with a redolence of meaning. Camels and gnats, fish and serpents, doves and roosters, rocks and mountains, rainbows and clouds, fire and lightning, brothers and sisters, Bethel and Babylon, the rich and poor, bread and wine— these are the staple items in Scripture's vocabulary. However, what they signify can be known only to the reader willing to ponder the reality they touch on. Speaking specifically of the Christian tradition but in a way that applies to the whole biblical tradition, Jung writes that the traditional religious symbol "is a living thing that carries in itself the seeds of further development. It can go on developing; it depends only on us, whether we can make up our minds to meditate again, and more thoroughly" on its premises.[24]

CHAPTER V

Biblical Archetypes and the Story of the Self

> Whoever speaks in primordial images speaks with a thousand voices;
> he enthrals and overpowers, while at the same time he lifts the idea
> he is seeking to express out of the occasional and transitory into the
> realm of the ever-enduring. He transmutes our personal destiny into
> the destiny of mankind, and evokes in us all those beneficent forces
> that ever and anon have enabled humanity to find a refuge from every
> peril and to outlive the longest night.
>   —"On the Relation of Analytic Psychology to Poetry"[1]

Once upon a time an old Persian king died, leaving his throne to
a young son. Calling the royal court together, the son asked each of
the courtiers how they planned to serve their new king.

"I am your councillor," said the first.

"I am your general," said the second.

"I am your chamberlain," said the third.

"I am your butler," said the fourth, and so on, through the hunts-
man, the footman, and the warden.

At the end of the line stood an old man who had said nothing.

"Who are you?" asked the king.

"I am your storyteller," replied the man.

"Storyteller indeed!" responded the young king. "Do you take me
for a child? I have no need of a storyteller!" He was about to order
the old man to be taken away, when the old man spoke up.

"What you have just told me, my Lord, is precisely what King

Dabzhelim told the wise man, Bidpai. In fact, the King threw Bidpai into the dungeon for his fables. But, the King soon recalled Bidpai when he realized he had been acting just like the blind man in the fable."

"What fable?" the young king barked.

The old man bowed and began to tell his story.

The purpose of this chapter is to ask why it is that certain stories exercise such power on the psyche and evoke such spontaneous response? One answer is found in Carl Jung's theory of the "archetypes." Jung suggests that in each of us there are structures of meaning and purpose that await arousal and expression, the content of which relates to who we are and what we are becoming. When a person appears with stories that touch these archetypal chords, he finds that they have the power to catalyze the mind, activate the will, and kindle the affections in ways that defy conscious expectation. We will explore Jung's theory of the archetypes and the light it casts on the power that the "old, old story" of Scripture continues to exercise in the psyche.

What Is an Archetype?

In his brief biography of Jung, Joseph Campbell writes:

> Already in 1909, but increasingly during his lonely and (as he knew) dangerous descent into the image producing abyss, he had been impressed by the recurrence of certain stereotypes among the figures of his dream-fantasies, suggesting those with which he was already acquainted through his studies of mythology. "I took great care," he states, "to try to understand every single image, every item of my psychic inventory, and to classify them scientifically . . . "; all of which led, finally, to his recognition of a cast of inevitable stock characters that have played through all time, through the dreams and myths of all mankind, in ever-changing situations, confrontations, and costumes. . . .[2]

Jung noted that these spontaneous images occurred not only in the delusional systems of the seriously disturbed but also in the dreams of ordinary people. Their presence could not be explained "by anything in the individual's own life"; rather, they seemed to be "aboriginal, innate, and inherited shapes of the human mind."[3] Jung tells of

ARCHETYPES

The archetypal motif of the unity of the masculine and feminine, the solar and the lunar, mediated by the descending dove-Spirit, as depicted in a sixteenth-century alchemical text.*

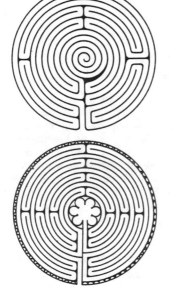

The archangel Michael subduing Satan, a bronze sculpture by Jacob Epstein on the front facade of the new Coventry cathedral in England, reflecting the recurrent motif of primordial struggle between good and evil, without and within.

The archetypal theme of life as journey and quest is captured in the image of the maze. The top figure represents a nineteenth century turf maze; the bottom, a tile maze on the floor of Chartres Cathedral, which was often walked by the pious as a symbolic pilgrimage to the Holy Land.

*Wellcome Institute, London. †Worcester Art Museum, Worcester, Massachusetts.

The archetypal theme of the "conjunction of the opposites" in Edward Hicks' painting of the Peaceable Kingdom of Isaiah 11:6–19, portraying the reconciliation of the red man and the white in William Penn's treaty with the Delaware Indians in 1682 (left) and the reconciliation of humankind and the "wild beasts," which Hicks once allegorized to mean the harmonization of the sanguine, choleric, phlegmatic, and melancholy sides of the self.†

The archetypal theme of death and rebirth is portrayed threefold in this fifteenth century woodcut, depicting (l. to r.) Joseph being lowered into the well, Christ being laid in the tomb, and Jonah being delivered to the great fish.

a professor who came to him one day in a state of panic reporting a sudden, baffling vision that made him doubt his sanity. Jung reports, "I simply took a 400-year-old book from the shelf and showed him an old woodcut depicting his very vision."[4] In such cases, Jung reports, "the most careful inquiry has never revealed any possibility of my patients' being acquainted with books or having any other information about such ideas. It seems that their unconscious mind has worked along the same line of thought which has manifested itself, time and again, within the last two thousand years."[5]

Jung writes:

> It was this frequent revision to archaic forms of association [in the dreams of his patients as well as the fantasies of schizophrenics] that first gave me the idea of an unconscious not consisting only of originally conscious contents that have got lost, but having a deeper layer of the same universal character as the mythological motifs which typify human fantasy in general. These motifs are not *invented* so much as *discovered*. They are typical forms that appear spontaneously all over the world, independently of tradition, in myths, fairytales, fantasies, dreams, visions, and the delusional systems of the insane. On closer investigation they prove to be typical attitudes, modes of action, thought processes and impulses which must be regarded as constituting the instinctive behaviour typical of the human species. The term I chose for this, namely "archetype," therefore coincides with the biological concept of the "pattern of behaviour." In no sense is it a question of inherited ideas, but of inherited, instinctive impulses and forms that can be observed in all living creatures.[6]

The Origin of the Term "Archetype." Jung introduced the term *archetype* in 1919, though at the same time experimenting with other phrases and terms, e.g., "primordial images," "structural dominants of the psyche," "the forms which instincts assume," "typical forms of apprehension," "inherited possibilities of representation," "a patterning force," a "system of readiness for action," and "the inner order of the unconscious."[7]

Jung finally settled on the term *archetype* because of its appropriate meaning ("primordial model") as well as its antiquity. Jung points out that the second-century Egyptian Gnostics were among the first to use the term, speaking of an "archetypal light" from which all other light derives. Irenaeus, Bishop of Lyons, proposed that God used "archetypes" or models when he created the world. The fifth-century neo-Platonic Christian, Dionysius the Areopagite, used the term *archetype* to distinguish a seal (model) from its impression (copy). Augustine's formulation of the concept, however, finally persuaded him. Writing in Latin around A.D. 400, Augustine defined the "archetypes" *(ideae principales)* as "certain forms" that "themselves do not perish, yet after their pattern everything is said to be formed that is able to come into being and perish."[8]

Characteristics of an Archetype. In his definition of "archetype" Jung emphasized several points. First, *he distinguished between the "archetype" and the "archetypal image."* The "archetypal image" is a specific expression of an archetype, e.g., a particular cultural or personal rendition of "the hero," or "the wise old man," or "the golden age." It is an "actualized archetype."

The archetype itself is not an image. It is the structural tendency within the human species to produce such images. Jung compared it to a negative that has to be developed, a primordial or latent image "determined as to its content only when it becomes conscious and is therefore filled out with the material of conscious experience."[9]

Second, *Jung regarded archetypes as inherent and universal in the human species.* They reside in the "bones and marrow" as deeply ingrained tendencies. Jung once described them as *engrams* or *imprints* on the soul that had developed like animal instincts as the result of innumerable, recurring experiences of the species adapting to its environment over the centuries.[10] Thus they are an "inherited mode of psychological functioning."[11]

"Although the specific shape in which they express themselves," Jung comments, will be

> more or less personal, the general pattern is collective. They are found everywhere and at all times, just as animal instincts vary a good deal in different species and yet serve the same general purposes. . . . They function, when the occasion arises, in more or less the same way in all of us.[12]

Jung regards it as a mistake to suppose the psyche of a newborn child is a *tabula rasa.*[13] As we are equipped to know how to suckle, breathe, eliminate, and cry, so we are equipped from the beginning with an apparatus of response to life that expresses itself along familiar, "archetypal" lines, wherever humans are found.

Third, *archetypes express themselves spontaneously and in a variety of forms.* The images they inspire are not the products of rational deliberation or decision. They appear to consciousness as irrational urges, e.g., to paint a certain picture, write a certain novel, compose a certain poem, choose a certain color, pursue a certain vocation, build a certain house, tell a certain story, or dream a certain dream.

The forms in which the archetypes express themselves are manifold. Commenting on the celebration of the universal hero myth, Jung notes that narration or storytelling is only one form in which this archetype is expressed. Other forms are utilized as well: worship service, dance, music, hymns, prayers, and sacrifice.[14] Archetypes can be rendered in "all typical, universally human manifestations of life, whether biological, psycho-biological, or spiritual-ideational."[15]

The Value of Archetypes

The archetypes, Jung tells us, provide "that character of apprehension or psychic grasp of situations which continually yield a further continuation of life"; they supply a "grasp of the momentary situation that perceives in it a meaning and purpose."[16] Archetypes enable us to go on. When our lives have taken a bad turn or when things are difficult, empty, or at a standstill, the archetypal structures of the psyche press on our consciousness to recognize a danger afoot or an opportunity at hand not previously considered.

Consciousness by its very nature, Jung tells us, tends to "concentrate on relatively few contents and to raise them to the highest pitch of clarity. A necessary result and precondition is the exclusion of other potential contents of consciousness. The exclusion is bound to bring about a certain one-sidedness of the conscious contents," taking one "further and further from the laws and roots of his being."[17]

Archetypes are compensatory to consciousness. When the mind doesn't know, the "gut" often does. When individuals or entire cultures have lost their way or turned a deaf ear to certain truths or options, an underground revolution takes place. The archetypes bombard consciousness with images and signals—in the conscience, in dreams, in the formation of complexes with repressed archetypes at their center, they will not be silenced.

The archetypes do not allow us to rest on our oars. They urge us to keep on beyond the narrow, pragmatic concerns of consciousness to the ideas, dreams, and convictions that give meaning and direction to life. "A sense of wider meaning to one's existence is what raises a man beyond mere getting and spending," Jung writes. "If he lacks this sense he is lost and miserable. Had St. Paul been convinced that he was nothing more than a wandering weaver of carpets, he certainly would not have been the man he was. His real and meaningful life lay in the inner certainty that he was the messenger of the Lord. One may accuse him of suffering from megalomania, but this opinion pales before the testimony of history and the judgment of subsequent generations."[18]

The archetypes are, in the end, the basis of all culture. Releasing the "hidden forces of instinct, to which the ordinary conscious will alone can never gain access,"[19] they provide the energy and set the dream to create cities, erect cathedrals, build bridges, plumb life's secrets, spawn the arts, and establish peace.

Types of Archetypes

"There are as many archetypes as there are typical situations in life."[20] Though Jung does not number or classify them, we will present some examples under two headings: archetypal persons, places, and things, perceived in the structure of experience; and archetypal processes perceived in the dynamics of experience.

Archetypal Persons, Places, and Things. This class represents figures that humans everywhere perceive as recurrent types. When we meet new persons we often perceive them in terms of these types and react accordingly. When we hear stories about these figures, we respond with the emotions we associate with these types.

The hero is the most psychologically powerful figure to appear in the art, literature, and storytelling of the world. Joseph Campbell's classic title, *The Hero with a Thousand Faces*,[21] makes this plain. Drawing on ancient sagas, stone reliefs, oral traditions, and wall paintings, from as far away places as Assyria and Babylon, Cambodia and Indonesia, Honduras and Argentina, Greece and Rome, he finds the hero, again and again, in a thousand guises.

We know his story well. Any one of us can construct it on demand: the twelve labors of Hercules, the tale of Gilgamesh, the travels of Odysseus, the lives of Moses and Abraham, the story of Jonah, the Way of the Cross. All relate to the three-fold pattern: *"the departure"* following a challenge or call; *"the trials"*; and *"the return,"* to everyone's astonishment. Not all heroes survive physically, nor are they all crowned. But all are tempered and not found wanting. The hero can appear as a warrior or lover, a prince or priest, a patriarch or prophet, male or female, a god or a human. But whenever his story is told, we listen:

> Once upon a time two friends, Ganem and Salem, set out on a journey. One day, near nightfall they came to a broad stream at the base of a wooded hill. Making their bed under the branches of an oak tree, they fell asleep, determined to cross the stream on the morrow.
>
> When they awoke, they saw a white stone by the side of the stream with a curious inscription:
>
>> Travelers, we have prepared an excellent banquet for your refreshment; but you must be bold and deserve it before you can obtain it. What you are to do is this: throw yourselves bravely into the stream and swim to the other side. You will find there a lion carved in marble. This statue you must lift upon your shoulders and, with one run, carry to the top of yonder mountain, never heeding the thorns which prick your feet nor the wild beasts that may be lurking in the bushes to devour you. When once you have gained the top of the mountain, you will find yourself in possession of great happiness.
>
> Ganem was delighted and suggested they try it. Salem, however, thought it a prank of some passing beggar. The current of the stream may run too swiftly for any man to swim. Perhaps the lion is too heavy to carry, if there is a lion! And it is impossible to think that anyone could reach the top of that mountain in one run. No, he would not go. So the two friends embraced and parted company.
>
> Stripping, Ganem dived into the stream. He found himself soon in a whirlpool. Using all his strength he made his way to the other side. When he was rested, he found the marble lion behind a clump of bushes. Lifting it to his shoulder and with one effort, he ran to the top of the mountain.
>
> At the summit he saw the gates of a beautiful city. As he stood looking, he heard a roar commencing from inside the lion! It grew

louder. Finally the turrets of the city trembled and Ganem saw great crowds pouring out of the gates. Unafraid of the noise, they came, led by a young nobleman, riding a black charger. Dismounting, he knelt before Ganem. "Brave stranger," he said, "we beseech thee to put on these regal robes and, mounted upon this charger, ride back with thy subjects to the city."

Ganem, astonished, asked how this could be. The young nobleman replied, "Whenever our king dies, we place by the river the stone with the inscription you have read. Then we wait patiently until a traveler passes by who is brave enough to undertake the bold venture. Thus we are always assured that our king is a man who is fearless of heart and dauntless of purpose. We crown you today as King over our city."[22]

When we hear such a story it is not important that the characters are fictitious; the story has authentic psychic weight and touches us with its transparent and compelling truth.

Archetypes of the masculine and feminine. The way we perceive men and women is affected by archetypes of the masculine and feminine. The masculine archetypes include the kind father as well as the ogre; the friendly dwarf and the ominous giant; the noble knight and the devilish trickster; the divine child and the youth savant; the wise man and the wizard; the saint and the sinner; the sage and the slayer of dragons; the frog with the prince inside and the tyrant king with a self-destructive demon inside.

The feminine archetypes manifest a parallel range: the nourishing mother and the cruel mother (more often than not, a "stepmother"); the lovely princess and the wicked queen; the wise old woman and the witch of the North; the heroine in armor and the Huntress; the virgin and the Earth Mother; Cinderella and the *femme fatale.*

Archetypes of the "inner self." We have noted earlier the four archetypes of the "inner self" Jung found most conspicuous: the persona, the anima/animus, the shadow, and the ego. Others might be added: the archetype of "flesh and spirit," often found at war with one another; the archetype of the androgyne, expressing the sense of a primordial unity of the sexes; the archetype of the "four humors," or in its modern Jungian version, the "four functions": thought, feeling, sense, intuition. They constitute a cast of figures recurring in literature touching on the inner life: morality plays, sermons, religious allegories, even psychiatric theories.

Archetypes of the "other." The Latin term *alienus* and the Greek term *barbaros* indicate the tendency to view a person of another tribe, religion, language, system, dress, custom, or land, in one of two stereotypical ways. One of the stereotypical reactions to an "other" is suspicion or fear. The central figure in Camus' *The Stranger* exemplifies this archetype. By the simple fact of his difference, he evokes a hostility that destroys him. Catholics and Protestants, Jews and Gentiles, whites and blacks have been seized by such archetypal feelings.

A second stereotypical reaction to the "other" is quite the opposite. It tends to see in the "other" a God-sent gift. "Do not neglect to show hospitality to strangers," the author of Hebrews writes; "for thereby some have entertained angels unawares" (Heb. 13:2). We find the same theme in Greek and Arabic culture. It even occurs in the American South in Peter Jenkins' autobiographical *A Walk Across America.* Taken under the wing of young, curious blacks in Murphy, North Carolina, Peter is introduced, with beard, Malamute, and backpack, to their mother, Mary Elizabeth. She, after a long but "loud" silence of studying and watching Peter as he eats his first meal in their trailer, tells him, "You don't know me yet, but I want ta tell ya something. . . . I believe in God. And I think He sent you here ta test aw faith. So, from now on, if you want to, you can stay with us."[23]

Archetypes of the cosmos. The word *cosmos* comes from a Greek root that means "structure" or "organization." Archetypes of the cosmos represent those typical ways in which persons through the ages have tended to formulate that structure. Has there ever been a culture that at one time did not think of its world in terms of a heaven above, the earth in the middle, and a realm of the demonic or dead below? Or has there ever been a culture that did not somewhere in its past divide the skies into zodiac-like constellations of stars that were seen not as mere lights but powers that affected human destiny? Even when "up" and "down" disappeared in the light of the space age, there were radio telescopes, space probes, and UFO watches still directed "out there" as the place from which "higher intelligence" could be expected.

Archetypes of the holy. The central archetype that springs up virtually everywhere, in every age, and at one time or another in every heart, is the holy archetype or God archetype. Though often expressed in spatial or temporal images, the God archetype urges us to think in terms beyond space and time, everywhere and yet nowhere, named and beyond naming, all good and yet finally encompassing all evil as well, the one and the many.

Like the "hero archetype," the holy archetype can be imaged in myriad forms. The trinitarian formulae suggests three categories of God images.

The holy can be imaged as spirit. This archetypal tendency urges us to consider the holy beyond humans and nature, rendered in images at best abstract: "the eternal," "the Platonic ideal," "the Logos" or "Word," "the Name," "heaven," "Being itself," or the *"mysterium tremendum et fascinosum."* It envisions the divine as beyond human structures, moving freely in and among us, invisible, incorporeal, yet bathing all it touches in ineffable power and light.

The holy can be imaged as a transcendent being with personal attributes. This archetypal tendency urges us to image the divine as transcendent but personal: a father, judge, master, creator, redeemer, with a face to turn toward us in blessing, an eye to observe our ways, an ear to hear our petitions, a strong arm to lift us up and guide us, and a voice to speak his word to his prophets. Though transcendent, he knows our nature and we are created in his image.

The holy can be imaged in incarnational terms, as God become human flesh. The experience of the early church catalyzed the most radical expression of this archetype, imaging God as become human, with a family, hometown, with arms, hands, eyes, ears, and a body of flesh, who ate, drank, wept, talked, became thirsty and fatigued, argued, taught, and after approximately thirty years of life, suffered and died as a public enemy. Judaism and Islam have resisted the expression of this archetype in such a radical form, restricting their portraits of God's immanence to images of prophets and teachers who are bearers of his word. Like Christianity, they have allowed that the holy can "descend" to touch special persons, places, or objects at special times, but they have avoided the absolutized image of the God-human union manifest in the Christian tradition.

IMAGES OF THE HOLY

The "hand" in Scripture commonly symbolizes power (Ps. 78:42), and frequently serves to symbolize the power and presence of the Holy in nature (Isa. 41:20), among his people (Exod. 6:1) and his prophets (Ezek. 1:3). The symbol appears often in Christian iconography as on this Irish high cross of Muiredach.**

Anthropomorphic images of God rarely capture the sense of cosmic mystery and power conveyed in William Blake's (1757-1827) "Ancient of Days" reflecting the words of Proverbs 8:27, "when he sets his compass upon the face of the deep."*

To temper a thoroughgoing anthropomorphism, some religious iconographers used only parts of the human body to portray the divine. Among them is the "eye of Providence" that dominates the reverse side of the Great Seal of the United States, set beneath the legend, "Annuit coeptis" ("He has favored our undertakings"). Adopted by the Continental Congress in 1782, the seal has appeared on the one-dollar bill since the administration of Franklin Delano Roosevelt.†

**Heather Child, Dorothy Colles, *Christian Symbols: Ancient and Modern*, copyright © 1971 Heather Child and Dorothy Colles. Reprinted with permission of Charles Scribners' Sons. *Fitzwilliam Museum; Cambridge, England. †Department of State; Washington, D.C. ‡Official Seal of The Jewish Theological Seminary of America. §Used by permission of Glencoe Publishing Co., Inc., from *Symbols in the Church*, second edition by Carl Van Treeck and Aloysius Croft. Copyright © 1936, 1960 by the Bruce Publishing Company. #Crucifix, Aus dem Wallis; photography by Swiss National Museum, Zurich.

Fire and flame appear consistently in religious traditions to symbolize the divine presence. Within Judaism, the burning bush (Exod. 3:2) has come to serve as a symbol of the divinely-ordered continuity in Jewish tradition and learning, which burns but is not consumed (cf. the illustration, which is the official seal of The Jewish Theological Seminary of America).‡

AND THE BUSH WAS NOT CONSUMED

והסנה איננו אכל

In the book of Revelation the victorious Lamb as the resurrected and exalted Christ symbolizes the ultimate victory of the power of meekness, innocence, purity, and holiness over against the power and force of evil.§

The power of the image of the crucified Christ to symbolize archetypal insights into the nature of the self and of the Holy is transparent in this twelfth-century Swiss wooden crucifix.#

The holy can be imaged in terms of nature, i.e., natural phenomena and creatures of the earth, sea, and sky. Christianity, Judaism, and Islam in general have resisted this archetypal tendency. To be sure, they will admit to images of the divine moving in wind or star, earthquake or storm; and we do hear in Scripture of a "whale," a lion in his den, or even the earth (Rev. 12:16) moving to do God's bidding, and of God's spirit descending in the form of a dove. But, in general, a theological consensus has developed to allow no sacred animal, stream, rock, or any other natural phenomenon into the imaginal repertory of the holy among the "religions of the Book." In fact, as a symptom of their disdain of the natural, they have tended to reserve natural and animal imagery for the demonic or Satanic: the dragons Leviathan and Rahab, the beast with 666 upon its forehead, and the talking serpent in the garden.

Archetypal Processes. The archetypal tendencies within us structure our perceptions of the world not only in terms of types of persons, places, and things in our inner and outer worlds, but also in terms of *processes.*[24]

The conflict between good and evil. In every culture at every level we find evidence of an archetypal preoccupation with the conflict between good and evil. It can be imaged in a thousand forms, but all are variations of a single perceptual motif, that life engages us in a battle between the light and the dark. Examples are the stories of the Lord subduing Leviathan in the Hebrew Scriptures, or of the Messiah overcoming the beast in Revelation, or of St. George subduing the dragon, David doing in Goliath, or of Robin Hood and the sheriff, or of the "white hats" and the "black hats" in Westerns, or of the Sons of Light and the Sons of Darkness in the writings of Paul and the Dead Sea Scrolls. In the heart of the London Zoo stands a tall statue in white stone, depicting a bare-chested male in mortal combat with a wild animal in attack position on its hind legs. The statue's power resides, not in its report of a famous fight between a man and an animal, but in its capacity to arouse in the viewer an archetypal openness to subduing the fiercest of forces, without or within.

Planting, growing, and harvesting. A compact parable in Mark's Gospel images the archetypal perception of planting, growing, harvesting as an analogue to the life process:

> The kingdom of God is as if a man should scatter seed upon the ground, and should sleep and rise night and day, and the seed should sprout and grow, he knows not how. *The earth produces of itself,* first the blade, then the ear, then the full grain in the ear. But when the grain is ripe, at once he puts in the sickle, because the harvest has come. (Mark 4:26–29, italics added)

The story in itself turns on the phrase, "the earth produces of itself," leading to the archetypal perception that the earth is a gracious mother (Latin *mater,* whence English "matter"), without whose rhythms and patterns we would not be sustained for a moment. But as a parable it occasions another archetypal insight, celebrated in Thanksgiving festivals and harvest ceremonies, that we live as part of a process in which we play at best a minuscule role, seeding, planting, perhaps watering a bit, but for the rest only waking and sleeping while the divine mysteries in nature move on.

Death and resurrection. The literature and art of the world reflect archetypal consciousness of another aspect of the divine mystery in life, namely death and resurrection. The subject matter is not just physical death and physical resurrection, but a pattern of being, in which what appears to be irreparable loss is supplanted by unimaginable gain: being hopelessly lost and then found, being hopelessly ill and healed, being hopelessly locked into a destructive pattern of living and then forgiven and released. The stories of the prodigal son, of the man blind from his youth, of the lost sheep, of the conversion of Paul, of the Exodus and Exile, of the Second Coming and the Last Day, and countless others, express this archetypal realization. Its liturgical analogue is found not only in the Easter celebration at the end of Holy Week, but in the ancient rite of baptism, which has at its heart the archetypal theme voiced in the words of Paul: "We were buried therefore with him by baptism into death, so that as Christ was raised from the dead by the glory of the Father, we too might walk in newness of life" (Rom. 6:4).

Experiencing life as history. Whenever one digs into the religious and philosophic traditions of the world, one finds a story, picture, or metaphysical model that reveals where time began, when it began, where it is heading, and what stages are in between. From Hesiod and his golden and silver ages, to Hegel with his historical sequence of thesis, antithesis, and synthesis, to the book of Revelation with its millennial schemes, we find expressions of the archetypal perception that history is real, and that the life story of humanity, of nations, and the world is neither blind nor shapeless. It respects a pattern of "ages," "epochs," "times and seasons," "millennia," or cycles that spell out a macrocosmic pattern within which the microcosm of our own time can and does play a role.

The Archetype of Archetypes: The Self

In his autobiography, Jung states that by 1920 he "began to understand that the goal of psychic development is the self, . . ." and that "the self is the principle and the archetype of orientation and meaning."[25] In David Cox's words, Jung concluded that the Self is a "sort of archetype of archetypes."[26]

The Self for Jung is, as noted earlier, not the ego. It is the Self with a large *s;* large not referring to one's ego but to the reality of a Self that is larger than ego.

The ego is the center of consciousness that thinks, plans, directs, and prides itself on these accomplishments. It is most visible in full form between childhood and middle age. It is the archetype of one's "subjective identity,"[27] with which we are wrapped up during the first half of life when we face the task of differentiating who we are. In the second stage of life, the Self begins to emerge more clearly into consciousness, with another task in hand. Not differentiation, but integration—integration and acknowledgement of all the parts of the self, even those the ego could never quite own up to: the persona, the shadow-side, the contra-sexual side, *all* one's attitudes and functions, not just one or two. The Self is the archetype of one's "objective identity"[28] in the sense of recognizing the broader reality of which we are part.

In Jung's own language, "the self designates the whole circumference which embraces all of the psychic phenomena in man. It expresses the unity and wholeness of the total personality. . . . Only partly conscious . . . , it embraces what can be experienced and what cannot or what has not yet been experienced."[29] Whatever the human's wholeness, or the Self, may mean *per se,* empirically it is an image of the goal of life spontaneously produced by the unconscious, irrespective of the wishes and fears of the conscious mind. It stands for the goal of the total person, for the realization of the person's wholeness and individuality with or without the consent of the will. "The dynamic of this process is instinct, which ensures that everything which belongs to an individual's life shall enter into it, whether he consents or not, or is conscious of what is happening to him or not."[30]

What images emerge in our art, literature, and dreams to express this archetypal perception of the Self? We have spoken of the mandala, which as a squared-circle in infinite variations expresses the inclusive as well as centered quality of the Self. "Hero stories" are also images of the Self, baiting the imagination and will to "win" our Selves, even at personal cost. Wise figures in fables and proverbs, like the tortoise and the ant, tutor us in truths about the Self from childhood. Poetry nourishes us with visions of the Self: "Two roads diverged in a wood and I, I took the road less travelled by." Parables abound with them: the pearl of great price; leaven hidden in a loaf; a mustard seed, so small in its beginning and so magnanimous in its maturity. The Gospels constantly return to the subject: "You are the salt of the earth; you are the light of the world," or, "What does a man gain by winning the whole world at the cost of this true self? What can he give to buy that self back?" Above all, God-images mirror the Self, as an expression of the immenseness of the mystery from which we are born, the heights to which we might aspire, and the depths we may have to plumb for the Self to come into its own. At the head of the list, in Jung's perspective, is the image of Christ, whom Jung says "exemplifies the archetype of the Self."[31]

Christ and the Self

In his 1952 essay *Answer to Job,* Jung wrote these words:

> Christ would never have made the impression he did on his followers
> if he had not expressed something that was alive and at work in their
> unconscious. Christianity itself would never have spread through the

pagan world with such astonishing rapidity had its ideas not found
an analogous psychic readiness to receive them.[32]

With these words Jung expresses the view that within every person
"there is an ever-present archetype of wholeness which may easily
disappear from the purview of consciousness or may never be perceived at all" unless it is awakened and illumined.[33] Jung suggests that
Jesus Christ occasions such an awakening and illuming by imparting
to the waiting "soul" an image of that Self for which it has always been
longing. In Jung's words, "Christ exemplifies the archetype of the
Self."

Jung is not alone in this proposal. Paul in the first century spoke
of the "Christ who lives in me," of the Christ "formed in you," and
of the Christ that "dwells in your hearts;" he also spoke of himself
as being "in Christ." Origen in the third century spoke of Christ as
the one "after whose likeness our inner man is made."[34] Karl Barth
in the mid-twentieth century, in a book entitled *The New Man,* writes:

> Jesus Christ is the secret truth about the essential nature of man.
> . . . Man's nature in Adam is not, as is usually assumed, his true and
> original nature; it is only truly human at all in so far as it reflects and
> corresponds to essential human nature as it is found in Christ. . . .
> The human nature of Christ is the final revelation of the true nature
> of man.[35]

What specifically does Jung have in mind when he speaks of Christ
as the exemplification of the archetype of the Self? Or what does Paul
mean when he speaks of "Christ in me" or I "in Christ?" What do
Origen and Barth intend with their formulations?

To answer these questions adequately, one would have to review
the testimony of the entire New Testament and twenty centuries of
Christian theology, piety, spirituality, morality, dogmatics, and art.
But it is possible to identify certain recurrent themes.

The Meaning of "Christ as the Image of the Self"

The Gospel of John cites a theme that serves as well as any to
epitomize what Christians find "in Christ." John professes that Christ
is *the Way, the Truth, and the Life.* For John these terms are virtually

synonymous, since the "way" that Jesus offers, *is* the "truth," and this "truth" brings "life."

Many other Christological titles emerge in the early church which express a similiar theme: Lord, Shepherd, Rabbi, Leader (Acts 5:31), Christ, and King. What they have in common is the confession that Christ is the one to rule in their hearts and to guide them on "the way."[36]

What sort of "way" is it? We can enumerate only a few of the motifs that surface again and again when Christians attempt to express what it means to be "in Christ."

The Way of a Servant. "Whoever would be great among you must be your servant" (Mark 10:43). With these words the Gospel touches on the major transformation of consciousness that Christ inspired in the psyche of the first-century world. As one theologian expressed it, "Christ took the *I* out of the center and replaced it with a *we.*" In psychological terms, it states that to become our Selves we must replace the *I* as the controlling sentiment in our lives with a broader consciousness of Self that links one's identity, one's wholeness, and one's fulfillment with that of one's neighbor.

The Way of Love. The Gospel of John reads: "By this all men will know that you are my disciples, if you have love for one another" (John 13:35). The teaching of Jesus detonated a lust for "love"; not the *eros* of acquisitive love, so native to the Greco-Roman psyche, but *agapē* that wills and does the best for another.

> The men of that age were ripe for identification with the word made flesh, for the founding of a community united by an idea, in the name of which they could love one another and call each other brothers. The old idea of . . . a mediator in whose name new ways of love would be opened, became a fact, and with that human society took an immense stride forward.[37]

The Way of the Spirit. We read in the Gospel of Mark that the one "unforgivable sin" is the "sin against the Holy Spirit"—indifference to its movements and resistance to its claims. The life of Christ is told as a "biography of the Spirit" from first to last: Christ is born of the

Spirit, driven into the wilderness by the Spirit, baptized in the Spirit; he preaches in the Spirit, in the end submits his Spirit to the Father, and extends the promise of the Spirit to his followers. New Testament Christians claim that the difference between themselves and others is an experience of having received the Spirit. This is not an experience of ecstatic bubbling, but, as Paul says, an experience of power—power to be, by God's grace, what one could not be on one's own. The proof is an inner transformation marked by the personal discovery that the power of selfishness, anger, jealousy, enmity, strife, dissension, envy, drunkenness, and carousing can be offset by the power of love, joy, peace, patience, kindness, goodness, faithfulness, gentleness and self-control (Gal. 5:19–22).

The Way of the Kingdom. Any first-century rabbi would have known what the "kingdom of God" is. It is that place where God rules in human hearts. According to the Gospels, the kingdom was the beginning and end of Jesus' teaching. The result was to inspire a new God-consciousness nourished by prayer, service, and acts of loving-kindness. The Parable of the Sower suggested that this sense of God's kingship would grow wherever his Word was sown. Jesus taught this; early Christians tried it; and later generations found it true.

The Way of Salvation. The New Testament words *salvation* and *savior* derive from a common Greek root that denotes the idea of "rescue," "healing," and "deliverance." The style of Jesus' ministry and his teaching suggest that "salvation" is high on the agenda: "saving" the ill with healing, "saving" the sin-ridden with forgiveness, "saving" the destitute with food and clothing, "saving" those in bondage through liberation, "saving" the lost by finding them. To be "in Christ" was not only to have experienced "salvation" in any or all of these forms, but to have undertaken the ministry of the "good news" of "salvation" oneself.

The Way of Reconciliation. We read in Paul's second letter to the Corinthians: "God was in Christ reconciling the world to himself . . . and entrusting to us the message of reconciliation" (2 Cor. 5:19). Though the word *reconciliation* does not occur in the Gospels, Paul found that the theme blazed like a torch in the life and ministry of Christ and ignited a fire in his own. For Paul "Christ was All and in All" (Col. 3:11). "Everything held together" in him (Col. 1:17). What this meant was that all the geographical, religious, social, ethnic, and racial divisions we impose on one another are broken down in Christ (Eph. 2:14). "There is neither Jew nor Greek, there is neither slave nor free, there is neither male nor female," Paul writes, "for you are all one in Christ Jesus" (Gal. 3:28). This conviction was inspired by the ministry of Christ, who embraced the Samaritan, conversed with the Gentile, ate with the tax collector and sinner, accepted the adulteress, approached the unclean, uplifted the poor, and loved the enemy. And in the end he foresaw the convergence of people from all over the world to God's final table, from South, North, East, and West (Luke 13:29). In a world conscious of its national, social, and class distinctions, this message of reconciliation dawned with archetypal power.

The Way of the Cross. We have spoken earlier of the "death and resurrection" theme as archetypal in the human psyche. It is echoed in the symbol of the "servant" Self, and is reiterated here. The cross does not develop as a Christian symbol until the fourth century. Its history as a symbol of cruelty and ignominy inhibited its earlier use in the church. But when it was finally adopted it had staying power, for it captured, among other truths, the realization that the cross was the place where the terror of history and the mystery of God meet. What appeared to be the end of the way was the beginning of a new way. Christian art expresses this by depicting the cross as a tree of life as well as a symbol of death. This theme, like the theme of the servant, restates the archetypal truth that it is only in giving the self away that the self is reclaimed. The story does not explain how this happens but simply stands as testimony to its truth and invites the hearers to assume this way for themselves.

The Christ-Event and the Life of the Soul

Having reviewed some of the key themes that spell out the meaning and content Christians find in the phrases, "Christ in me" or "Christ as an image of the Self" or "Christ as the true nature of humankind," the question remains how this reality is communicated to another. How does the transaction take place? How is the image of Christ awakened in the believer?

Rudolf Bultmann, the foremost New Testament scholar in the early and mid-twentieth century, employed the phrase "Christ-event" to refer to the transformation Jesus occasioned in the lives of Christians. For Bultmann, the "Christ-event" was a "Word-event." Without explaining the mechanism, Bultmann saw the speaking of the Word and the hearing of the Word as the point-of-contact between Christ and the believer.

In the history of Christian thought and practice the point-of-contact has been located in other places. Some have proposed the point-of-contact is in the *sacraments;* others, in confessing the *creed;* others, in the *imitation of Christ.* For Jung, the point-of-contact is in the soul. There can be a sacramental dimension, a creedal dimension, an "imitative" dimension, but the locus of the event is the soul. It is the "soul" the Word touches, not just the mind. It is the soul the sacrament nourishes, not just the body. It is the wisdom of the soul the creeds confess, not just that of the rational intellect. It is to the whole soul that the rhythms of the "Savior" appeal as a beat worth imitating, not just to the conscience.

What is the soul? As we have noted earlier, it is the totality of the conscious and unconscious Self, the seat of our perceptions and powers, intellectual and moral, spiritual and sensual. It is the place where the dark and light sides coexist and where the hopes and memories, aspirations, and archetypal longings stir. Jung spoke of it as "a part of the inmost mystery of life. . . . I can only gaze [at it] with wonder and awe."

When Jung speaks of Christ as the exemplification of the archetype of the Self, he is referring to an event in the life of the soul. This Christ-Event not only "speaks" to the soul, it "acts" upon it, awakening, reviving, cleansing, nourishing, resurrecting. Its effects, in time, take on visible expression in the form of writing, ritual, dogma, creed, sacrament, painting, inscription, homily, and lifestyle.

The appearance of Jesus of Nazareth in the first-century Greco-Roman world "expressed something," as Jung observed, "that was alive and at work" within the soul. The "good news" spread because there was a "psychic readiness" to receive it. Those who were touched by it had not known what they were looking for until it arrived. When it did, they recognized it. As an anonymous fifteenth-century poet observes for us:

> Thou shalt know Him when He comes
>   Not by any din of drums—
>   Nor the vantage of His airs—
>   Nor by anything He wears—
>   Neither by His crown,
>   nor His gown.
> For His presence known shall be
>   by the Holy Harmony
> That His coming makes in thee.

Why Scripture Speaks

Scripture is in part the product of its original authors, who wrote out of their own experience and enlightened wisdom. The prophets, Paul, the authors of the Gospels, all wrote with data supplied them as refracted through the lens of the Word that seized them.

Scripture is also the product of later generations of Hebrews and Christians who, reading the words of the prophets, apostles, and evangelists, heard a Word themselves. In response to the Word they gathered these writings into a canon of "sacred books," a collection of writings, that did not differ from many other books of their times generically, but spiritually had the power to address the mind and assault the soul in ways that other literature did not.

They gathered Scripture, inspired by the Spirit that addressed them through it, and created the text of a "holy Bible," a soul book. It consisted of an array of laws, psalms, legends, myths, prophecies, parables, riddles, letters, gospels, historical accounts, and apocalypses. But in its pages was a treasury of archetypal motifs related to the life of the soul that could challenge the mind, comfort the troubled spirit, warm the heart, sensitize the conscience, strengthen the will, enlarge the vision, and deepen the awareness of the holy. They gathered it because they knew it had the power to speak and that its preservation alone would insure that generations of souls hence would have access to its voice and find in it a Word to awaken and even "save" their souls.

For Jung, as for these gatherers of Scripture, the power of the text lies in its ability to address the soul, as Jung writes:

> Whoever speaks in primordial images speaks with a thousand voices; he enthrals and overpowers, while at the same time he lifts the idea he is seeking to express out of the occasional and transitory into the realm of the ever-enduring. He transmutes our personal destiny into the destiny of mankind, and evokes in us all those beneficent forces that ever and anon have enabled humanity to find a refuge from every peril and to outlive the longest night.[38]

CHAPTER VI

Letting the Bible Speak: A Jungian Approach to Biblical Interpretation

> The eternal truths cannot be transmitted mechanically; in every epoch they must be born anew from the human psyche.
> —*After the Catastrophe*[1]

In *The Wounded Healer*, Henri Nouwen tells the tale of a young fugitive who comes to a town where the people are willing to take him in. When soldiers arrive seeking the fugitive, the townspeople admit to knowing nothing about him. Suspecting their lie, the soldiers warn that unless the fugitive is turned over by morning, the entire town will be burned. In deep consternation the people rush to their pastor for counsel.

The pastor, greatly troubled, retreats to his study to search the Scriptures. All night he reads, but finds nothing. Just before dawn his eye falls on a passage: "It is better that one man should die for the people than that a whole people be lost." The minister goes to his people with the news of his discovery. The soldiers are informed and the young man is taken away. A great festival commences, lasting far into the night, celebrating their miraculous deliverance.

But the pastor returns to his study, still troubled. That night an angel appears to him. "Why are you troubled?" the angel asks. "Because I have turned the fugitive over to the enemy," he replies. "But did you not know that he was the Messiah?" the angel inquires. "How was I to know?" the pastor replies in great anguish. The angel responds, "If, instead of reading your Bible you had visited the young man and looked into his eyes, you would have known."[2]

The tragedy of this story turns on the question, "How are we to understand Scripture correctly?" In this instance, the book of life became a book of death because it was wrongly understood. On other occasions, for the same reason, the book of freedom has become a book of slavery; the book of grace has become a book of condemnation; the book of soul has become a book of religious facts.

What we hear in Scripture depends on how we understand Scripture. Therefore it is important, before we undertake the task of interpreting Scripture, to come to a decision on several key questions: "What is the Bible?" "Who am I, the reader?" "Who is he, the author?" and given this, "How am I to approach this book?" Although Carl Jung has not addressed all these questions systematically, he has, in the length and breadth of his writings, provided a perspective on these questions consonant with the insights of many contemporary biblical scholars, theologians, psychologists of religion, pastors, and spiritual directors—Roman Catholic, Jewish, and Protestant—pointing to a way of reading Scripture today.[3]

What Is the Bible?

A new perspective that is developing on the question "What is the Bible?" can be expressed in the form of seven propositions touching on traditional and familiar issues. Each deserves fuller treatment than is possible here, but together they hint at a new consensus that is developing concerning the nature and purpose of Scripture.

First, it is becoming clear to biblical theologians that *the Bible is a book in which the focal point lies outside itself.* The Bible does not point to itself, it points beyond itself, to God, to neighbor, and to self. It was on this point that Jung differed from his pastor father. Jung saw in his father's veneration of Scripture the tendency to relate to the Bible rather than to life and to the God in the midst of life. For his father the Bible was a guide to theology and orthodoxy. For Jung the Bible was a guide to life and to God-consciousness.

The New Testament tells of a similar attitude among the religious leaders and interpreters of Scripture in Jesus' day. Jesus tells them, "You search the scriptures, because you think that in them you have eternal life" (John 5:39). From Jesus' standpoint, eternal life is not in the Book; it is in the people and events and voices outside the Book through which God is constantly speaking and to which Scripture points. They were under the impression that the bottom line in Scripture was the text itself. For Jesus, the bottom line was the presence of the living God, to whom the text unerringly points and to whom it constantly seeks to draw our attention. As a contemporary Benedictine comments, "We do not stop at the word God speaks, but at the God who speaks his word."[4]

A second point, realized increasingly by biblical scholars, is that *the Bible intends to address the present reader, even though it originates in the past.* This should not surprise anyone who has read Plato, Shakespeare, Thomas Jefferson, or Mark Twain. Not one of them meant their words for their original readers only. They were all addressing anyone in any generation who might be interested in their ideas. St. Paul takes the Hebrew Scriptures this way. "Whatever was written in former days was written for our instruction," he tells us in Romans 15:4. The stories of Adam, Noah, and the patriarchs, as Jung concurred, were intended for more than a one-night run. Their story is our story. And the words written about Abraham in Genesis, Paul tells us again, were written not for Abraham's sake alone "but for ours also" (Rom. 4:23–24).

A third proposal Jung and others would make about Scripture is that *the Bible is not the words of God, but the Word of God.* Historical criticism has impressed us indelibly with the truth that the words of Scripture are the words of their scriptural authors. It is through *their words,* and through their grammar and syntax, that *the Word* is refracted.

This is plain in Scripture itself. When John speaks of the Word become flesh or when Paul prays for a door to be opened for the Word, neither has in mind the 773,692 *words* of the English Bible, not to mention the corresponding number in the Hebrew and Greek originals. The Bible may refer to itself as the Word of God (e.g., Mark 7:13), but never as the *words* of God.[5]

What is the Word of God according to Scripture? It can be the

Word addressing a prophet, the Word preached, the Word that goes forth from the mouth of the Lord to accomplish his will and much more. In every instance the phrase refers to the power and presence of God at work in his world, not to words about him.[6]

A fourth related observation about Scripture, which Protestantism finally is beginning to accept, is that *the Bible is not the only locus in which God's speaking can be heard.* As Jung points out, the peculiar notion that God speaks only in Scripture is a product of the Reformation. In reaction to the Roman teaching of "no salvation outside the church" (*extra ecclesiam nulla salus est*), the Protestants responded with the equally stringent doctrine of "by Scripture alone" (*sola scriptura*).[7]

The restriction of God's speaking to the pages of a book or to the pages of the past is repugnant to Scripture itself. Nowhere in Scripture is God ever conceived of as one who expresses himself primarily in print. He is to be found in the storm, in the whirlwind, in the cataclysmic events of history, in the healing presence of his Son, in the ongoing proclamation of the church. For Paul, the prophets, the Gospel writers, and the spirit-baptized Christians, it was unthinkable to suggest that God's speaking could ever be restricted to written form and it is their ongoing expectation that God continues to speak and manifest his will through the power and presence of his spirit, in all ages and in all times.

A fifth observation Jung would take as self-evident about Scripture is that *although the Bible is the church's Book, insight into its Word is by no means limited to confessing believers.* Thomas Merton echoes this sentiment.

> The believer should not cling too complacently to his status and apparent privilege, as if the Bible were *his* book exclusively and as if *he* knew all about it. . . . The Bible is everybody's book and the unbeliever can prove himself as capable as anyone else of finding new aspects of it which the believer would do well to take seriously.

In fact, Merton observes, non-believers "are sometimes in a better position to enter into dialogue and struggle with the Bible than believers themselves."[8]

Merton cites as an example the Marxist film writer Pasolini, who, marooned in an Assisi hotel because of a traffic jam occasioned by a visit of Pope John XXIII, picked up a hotel copy of the Gospel of Matthew and read it for the first time in his life. This event inspired his epic film, *The Gospel According to St. Matthew.*

As a sixth point, concerning the doctrine of scriptural inspiration, it is well to note that when the Bible speaks of Scripture as "inspired," it says nothing about inerrancy or infallibility. *The doctrine of scriptural inspiration points to the special origin, character, power, and purpose of Scripture.* Jung observes, "We cannot explain an inspiration. Our chief feeling about it is that it is not the result of our own ratiocinations, but that it came to us from elsewhere."[9]

The key New Testament text on scriptural inspiration is 2 Timothy 3:16–17, which in the RSV reads: "All scripture is inspired by God and profitable for teaching, for reproof, for correction, and for training in righteousness, that the man of God may be complete, equipped for every good work." When we look at the passage in toto and when we examine the Greek text we note two important facts. First, reading the verse in its broader context we see that the point the author wants to get across is not the *fact* of an inspired text but the *purpose* of an inspired text, namely "to equip the man of God for every good work."

The second fact we observe is that the Greek word for "inspiration" is *theopneustos,* meaning "God-breathed." To say that "all Scripture is *theopneustos*" is to affirm that it is the product of God's breathing in the heart and hand of the author, and that those who read these words will come away refreshed and nourished by that same spirit. Inerrancy is not the issue, but rather the unmistakable presence we feel breathing through the words as we read and meditate on them.

Finally, a point central to Jung's understanding and use of the Bible is that *the ultimate purpose of Scripture is not information but transformation.* The story is told of a woman on a mission field sitting under a tree reading the Bible. A friend passes by and asks, "What book are you reading?" She responds, "I'm not reading this book. This book is reading me." The men and women who gathered Paul's letters, the Gospels, the Hebrew Scriptures, the later epistles, and the Apocalypse to form the Christian Bible would agree. They acknowledged that the Bible served some historical interest; it was a helpful worship resource; it was indispensable for teaching; it informed belief.

But the paramount purpose of Scripture is the transformation of the reader. The ordination service of a deacon in the Roman Catholic Church today highlights this aim in one of the ordination prayers:

> May you believe what you read;
> May you proclaim what you believe;
> May you become what you proclaim.

Who Am I, the Reader?

Karl Barth observes that we often come to Scripture with the question "What is this book?" but discover that this book asks us, "Who is this that reads it?"[10] This question lies at the heart of Jung's life and work as well as that of the entire psychological and psychoanalytic tradition. Modern psychology was not the first to raise a call to self-knowledge. Socrates, in repeating the Delphic maxim, "Know Thyself," had said it quite explicitly. The book of Proverbs taught it on every page. Augustine, with typical psychological shrewdness, observed among other things that "before God can deliver us we must undeceive ourselves." The only advantage of modern psychology is that it issues the summons in new garb. The point is clear: before engaging in any enterprise, including the study of Scripture, it is important to know who you are and what you bring to the task.

Some wry sage commented that when a monkey looks into a mirror he will see a monkey staring back at him. Barth echoed this insight with the observation that "the Bible gives to every man and to every era such answers to their questions as they deserve."[11] The admonition applies even to the biblical scholar who, despite his claims to unbiased objectivity, "carries the shell of an inherited tradition about him just as much as a citizen of the ancient world."[12] Each of us carries a special tradition, a set of values, a list of personal problems, a well-seasoned world-view, a set of tailor-made complexes, and a large dose of humanity, wherever we go and to whatever task we undertake.

When we approach Scripture we come with this same baggage. It is not possible to come in any other way. But Jung and Scripture itself would tell us that it is best to know what we bring and how it may affect our reading for good or ill. No message comes through more clearly in Jung's entire career than the importance of coming to know and coming to terms with "what lies under the hood." In his judgment, those persons who lack that awareness, and who do not recognize, as Jesus taught, that it is out of our own hearts that evil, murders, adulteries, thefts, false witness and a host of other vices proceed, are the persons most apt to unleash the excesses—pogroms, witch-hunts, heretic burnings, and crusades—in the name of Scripture. It is important when approaching Scripture to have as clear a bead as possible on "who this is who reads," for the protection of others, for the protection of Scripture, and for our own protection.

Who Are They, the Authors?

Aside from the theory held by one New Testament scholar that the book of Hebrews was written by a woman, it seems likely that the biblical authors are hes and not shes. But even this fact is not so important for getting at what the authors have to give. Nor do we need to be absolutely certain about their birthplaces, nationalities, or occupations. As exciting as it can be to track down vital statistics on biblical authors, the yield is modest with respect to our main task of understanding what it is that Scripture wants to tell us.

What we do want to know about the authors of Scripture is what makes them write the way they do and what realities, truths, and insights they want to share with us. To answer these questions we need to do some historical-critical work to understand where the authors stand within the religious, cultural, and political climate of their own time and place. But we also need to be helped by the sister discipline of psychology to remind us, as Jung puts it, that "humanity is one, with one psyche,"[13] and that biblical authors were traveling the same route we are, from childhood to middle and old age, moved by the same archetypal needs and longings. Genetics will tell us we are by no means clone-models of one another, and psychology will show our psychic makeups to be different. But, despite these differences, one basis for our engaging in conversation with these authors, so far removed from us in time and space, is a fundamental affinity of soul, marked by a common archetypal drive toward wholeness and toward the holy.

Psychological and theological criticism will also help us understand what it is we can expect to get from such authors. They are not writing primarily because they are scholars, essayists, historians, or poets, but because they are individuals whose lives have been touched by the numinous and because they live in a community of persons who share that experience. The nature of the transaction between those ancient authors and ourselves is less a matter of data-transfer than what might be called spirit-transfer. Their hope, even at this distance, is that through some alchemy of soul the Word that burns in their hearts and their communities might kindle a flame in ours.

Some Jungian Guidelines for Interpreting Scripture

We noted earlier Jung's acknowledgment that he does not write as a biblical scholar "but as a layman and a physician who has been privileged to see deeply into the psychic life of many people." Jung accordingly presents no method of biblical interpretation. But he does propose an approach to literature, the arts, dreams, and other "texts" of the soul that can be of help to biblical interpreters in approaching Scripture.

Jung's approach to any of these texts, whether a dream "text" or a scientific treatise, differs from that of the historical-critical. Jung does not dismiss such an approach. His work demonstrates keen interest in the historical circumstances surrounding a text, the author's background, the lexical, grammatical, and syntactic idiosyncrasies of the text, the author's purpose, the audience he addresses, and the literal meaning of the text. But his primary objective is to raise the question, "What is the significance of this text in the life of the soul?"

To pry open an answer to this question, Jung developed two hermeneutical or analytic-interpretive techniques, called *amplification* and *active imagination*. Though originally applied to the interpretation of dream "texts," they are also useful in the "investigation of psychologems, mythologems, and psychic structures of all kinds."[14] For our purposes they suggest a manner of approaching Scripture.

Amplification. Jung developed the method of amplification in connection with his work of assisting patients to understand the symbols, images, and themes of their dreams. Dreamers were first asked how their dreams impressed them, what seemed most significant, and whether it was agreeable or not. Second, the dreamers were led into a process of "directed association," namely, to track down every association they might have with each of the dream images toward the end of identifying what particular meaning the images held for them.

Amplification proceeded at two levels, the subjective (or personal) level and the objective (or collective). At the subjective level the dreamers focused on what the dreams meant to them personally. But in some instances images appeared that the dreamers had no experience of at all. They might be mythical, phantasmagoric, or cosmic in nature. In this case Jung would proceed with *objective amplification,* drawing on his knowledge of mythology, anthropology, folklore, legend, ethnology, and religious tradition to reveal to the dreamers how some of the very themes that appeared so puzzling and exotic in their dreams have, in fact, been known elsewhere in the literature and art of the world and have to do with an element of the archetypal agenda common to humanity.

In summary, amplification is the "elaboration and clarification of a dream-image by means of directed association and of parallels from the human sciences (symbology, mythology, mysticism, folklore, history of religion, ethnology, etc.)."[15] Its goal is "to comprehend the symbolic significance and the archetypal roots of a dream, fantasy, hallucination, painting, or any other human product."[16]

For the scriptural interpreter, whose task it is to amplify the meaning of the biblical text for the modern reader, there is no access, of course, to the personal meaning the text might have had in the life of the biblical author. But the interpreter can explore the meanings of the text in the personal life of the reader as well as comment on its "collective" or "objective" ramifications.

To amplify the meaning of the text at the *personal or subjective level,* one would first read the text carefully and then attempt to identify, out of all the associations one has with the various images and themes, which of them speaks most clearly to one's personal situation. Bible study groups have commonly employed this method of subjective or personal amplification in corporate examination of the text that leads to the recognition of associations and meanings that might otherwise never have come to consciousness.

To amplify the text at the *objective or collective level* requires, as in the case of dream interpretation, the help of someone professionally familiar with the stages and seasons of the soul and with the archetypal motifs that play on it. The function of the scriptural interpreter when dealing with these archetypal motifs is to amplify their meaning with a comparative symbology drawn from the rich treasury of the church's experience as well as from the mythic and religious traditions beyond. Within the church, this function of providing an objective or collective amplification of the archetypal motifs in Scripture has been that of the preacher and the teacher. Their vocation is to illustrate how the great themes of Scripture are echoed in the great themes of the church as they bear on the role of the individual and the community within the context of the whole human story and within the purview of the "divine plan."

More generally, the process of amplification suggests the need to take time with the text, to listen to it, and to explore its range and depth of meaning, attentive to details, and sensitive to its polyvalent themes. Amplification technique reminds us that a scriptural image, story, or symbol may have a depth of meaning of which the author and even earlier readers are unaware. Jung cites the common experience of the poet who "thinks he knows what he is saying but actually says more than he is aware of."[17] Thus it is conceivable that Isaiah or Paul, Ezekiel or the author of Revelation may at times have uttered images which far outreach their awareness, coming to rest years and even centuries later in the soul of a reader who perceives their previously unrecognized depths. It was precisely such an insight, stressing the polyvalence of the revealed Torah, that led the rabbis to propose that there are two laws, the written law and the oral law, the latter continuing to come to light over the centuries as the students plumb the depths of the written law. Within the Roman Catholic tradition, the same amplificatory function is seen at work in the development of dogma as the elaboration of truths inherent but not originally perceived in the primordial revelatory event. The themes that are discovered through amplification of the text echo meaningfully, not only with respect to the microcosmic world of the individual but also on the macrocosmic aspect of one's journey and one's role within the broader context of meaning and mystery to which Scripture continually draws our attention.

Active Imagination. Unlike amplification, which aims at the clarification of a dream image, active imagination aims at its expression in a new medium, in visual or audible form. Jung captures the essence of active imagination in his widely quoted statement: "The most we can do is to dream the myth onwards and give it a modern dress."[18]

For Jung the unconscious is the repository of the imagination, from which fantasies, visions of the future, new ideas, and insights emerge. They lurk there, so to speak, in potentiable form, springing to life when the one-sidedness of consciousness calls for their compensatory presence. The unconscious manifests itself in its most unadulterated form in our dreams. But dreams are not always as transparent to the "intention" of the unconscious as we would like. In such instances Jung recommended the use of active imagination, inviting the patient to draw out the unconscious content through the exercise of the imagination expressed in concrete form, e.g., a drawing, a painting, clay modeling, dance, free writing, storytelling or spontaneous fantasies.[19] By means of this strategy, the conscious side of the self was enlisted to coax the unconscious side into expressing some of its undisclosed content, so that it might be brought into the daylight of consciousness and used as a resource in coping with the problems of the day. As Jung observes, "often the hands know how to solve a riddle with which the intellect has wrestled in vain."[20]

What one discovers in the practice of active imagination is how surprising a resource it is. E. A. Bennet tells us, for example, that we may start a painting, a design, a carving, or a poem "with no end in view, and then it begins to take shape, form and thereby comes alive, and does express something that cannot be expressed in words."[21] Jung maintains we rely on this hidden unconscious resource to a greater extent than we realize. Even in everyday conversation we are surprised by "the admirable (or regrettable) ideas that appear in our minds 'from nowhere'—our way of describing the unconscious."[22] The surprising thing is that these ideas that "come into our heads" often throw a new light on everyday problems. Active imagination enables us to stir these subliminal contents and to summon at least some of them up top for inspection. Painting the picture or modeling clay can be like a "voyage of discovery into the inner world of the psyche. On the way, moods, previously puzzling, can be apprehended because their meaning has been felt, seen in a flash—a flash of intuitive understanding."[23]

Active imagination as a technique for getting in contact with the unconscious depth of the self is regarded as one of Jung's most important discoveries. It echoes what Augustine knew about the soul, that it was a *thesaurus inscrutablis,* an unfathomable treasury of ideas: "When I enter there," Augustine writes, "I require instantly what I will to be brought forth, and something instantly comes; others must be long sought after . . . others rush out in troops . . . these I drive away with the hand of my heart . . . until what I wish for be unveiled."[24] It also has affinities with the techniques of Zen Buddhism and Tantric Yoga in the East and the Ignatian Exercises and centering prayer in the West, all of which acknowledge the inscrutable but rich resource of the imagination.

The technique of active imagination has long-standing relevance for the scriptural interpreter. Though the church never called it by name, it has long practiced the art of active imagination by inviting its musicians and playwrights, its artists and liturgists, its homilists and teachers, to turn to their imaginations to find new ways and new forms for expressing scriptural truths. Active imagination reminds the scriptural interpreter that the truth of a text can be conveyed in manifold forms, objective and non-objective art, visual and plastic arts, verbal and non-verbal expression, musical or dance forms, in a poem, novel, story, or play. It further reminds the scriptural interpreter that each of these forms represents a curiously discreet angle of vision which, because of its peculiar character, can perceive and draw things out of the text other faculties and modes of expression would never catch. Active imagination refuses to play in one key or on a single instrument of the psyche; it experiments with the whole range of the soul's instrumentation, demonstrating how each catches and voices the message in a special way.

Together the techniques of amplification and active imagination suggest two necessary ingredients in approaching Scripture as a text for the soul: the art of listening to the text carefully and fully and the art of interpreting its meaning with the use of all the arts the imagination can muster.

Amplification and the Art of Listening to Scripture

A Jungian amplification of Scripture as a text with polyvalent depths, addressing the self both in its personal and collective modalities, would emphasize the need for listening—thoughtfully, empathetically, broadly, wholly, and prayerfully.

Listening Thoughtfully. The interpretation of a dream "text" requires attention to detail. We must amplify every element of a dream, Jung contends, "if we are to form a total picture from which the meaning can be deciphered."[25] The same holds true when we approach Scripture. It is easy to read Scripture quickly, without thinking, because the words are so familiar. But to do so is to miss much.

Mark Link, who understands so well what Scripture holds, reminds us of the reading technique Sidney Piddington recommends in "The Special Joys of Super-Slow Reading." Piddington developed the technique in a Japanese prisoner-of-war camp in Singapore. Just before his capture he stuffed a copy of Lin Yutang's *The Importance of Living,* his only book, in his knapsack. Piddington tells us,

> Finally, as the sun went down one evening, I walked out into the prison yard, sat down on a pile of wood and, under the glare of prison lights, slowly opened the book to the title page and frontispiece. I spent three sessions on the preface, then two whole evenings on the contents page—three and a half pages of chapter headings with fascinating subtitles—before I even reached page one.

After two weeks he was only on page ten.

> I began to realize how much I was getting from super-slow reading itself. Sometimes just a particular phrase caught my attention, sometimes a sentence. I would read it slowly, analyze it, read it again—perhaps changing down into an even lower gear—and then sit for 20 minutes thinking about it before moving on. . . . The realization dawned on me that although my body was captive, my mind was free to roam the world.[26]

Taking time enabled him to reach into the depths of the book. It also allowed the book to seep into the tissue of his own soul.

Listening Empathetically. Understanding the special perspective of a patient places a great demand on the therapist, Jung tells us. It is not enough to be an observer; one must be a "fellow participant" in a process encompassing both.[27]

So in approaching Scripture, it is not enough to be objective. One must cultivate an approach of *empathy* to understand what the authors have to tell us. "Understanding" means standing "with" and "under" those whose word we wish to comprehend. It means pondering *their* perspective, asking *their* questions with them, venturing *their* dreams, and wrestling with the issues *they* are grappling with. To understand Scripture means to amplify our perceptions with the perception of the biblical authors, who like ourselves, understand themselves to be part of a story being told by the divine.

Listening Broadly. For more than nineteen centuries the Bible has struck a spark in thousands of minds in thousands of ways, and neither the number nor the effect has been limited to professional biblical scholars. Painters, sculptors, liturgists, spiritual directors, theologians, musicians, playwrights, poets, novelists, preachers, saints, pastors, architects, hymn writers, missionaries, politicians, philosophers, popes, and bishops with an infinite assortment of butchers, bakers, and candlestick makers, male and female, have been moved to response by the Word. St. Teresa and Jacob Epstein, Shakespeare and Kazantzakis, Michelangelo and St. John of the Cross, Marcion and Kierkegaard, Schleiermacher and Teilhard de Chardin, Augustine and Rahner, Aquinas and Tillich, Fulton Sheen and Billy Graham, Pasolini and DeMille, St. Francis and Albert Schweitzer, Martin Luther and Martin Luther King, Jr., John XXIII and Karl Barth, Gen. William Booth and John Wesley, along with thousands of preachers, biblical commentators, tellers of biblical stories and common biblical readers—all have been moved to respond to Scripture. They have come to its pages from a thousand points of departure and have heard the Word in as many different keys.

Listening to Scripture in our time involves listening to what others have heard in their times. Often the tones will match. But just as often we discover sounds we have missed. The hearing of the past is a treasury for the present, enabling us to detect a broader registration of sound that can be struck from Scripture. It is cheering as well as chastening to suspect there are sounds we have yet to hear.

Listening Wholly. One of the most important lessons Jung has to teach contemporary Western humanity is that understanding requires more than rational thought. Jung's theory of the four functions proposes that we come to the truth by thinking, to be sure, but by sensing, feeling, and intuiting, as well. We come to the truth in Scripture in the same four ways.

Scripture certainly requires *thinking*. To comprehend the wisdom of the Proverbs, to follow the tortuous rabbinic arguments of Paul, to untangle the kings of Israel and Judah, or to understand a difficult passage or phrase demands thinking. But there are some truths in Scripture that refuse to yield to thought alone; they require other faculties to be comprehended.

Without the faculty of *sense,* the love scenes in the Song of Solomon, the references to Mt. Tabor and Mt. Hermon, the allusions to the lily of the field, the starry heavens, the wine that gladdens the heart, the oil that makes the face shine, and the bread that strengthens the heart would make little or no sense. Nor would the stories of the demoniac shrieking among the tombs, the three crosses on the hill, and the sparrow fallen to the ground. The incarnation itself loses power when it is only an idea. It became an "idea" eventually, but it began as a truth the sense first knew when the disciples ate, walked, and lived with the man Jesus and touched his flesh.

The *feeling* function is indispensable to scriptural understanding. The prophet Micah does not appeal primarily to rational thought nor to the senses when he tells us, "He has shown you, O man, what is good, and what does the Lord require of you, but to do justice, and to love kindness, and to walk humbly with your god." The appeal is comprehensible only to that side of the self that distinguishes right from wrong, good from evil, the whole from the ill. Most of Scripture, certainly the prophets and Jesus, aim at arousing the feeling function, inviting us not to become merely intellectually alive or sensually alive but morally alive, and to turn to consider what is true, honorable, just, pure, lovely, gracious, excellent, and worthy of praise (Phil. 4:8). A folk saying comments on the wisdom that feeling can have over intellect: "There are some things in the Bible I can't possibly understand; there are some things in the Bible I think I understand; and there are some things in the Bible I can't possibly misunderstand."

The *intuitive* function underlies all biblical understanding. Keeper of the sixth sense and inner vision, the intuitive dares to venture beyond the empirical, to speak of that which neither ear has heard nor eye seen. Paul's faith en route to Rome in chains, Isaiah's vision in the sanctuary of the temple, and the Psalmist's confidence in the valley of the shadow of death are unthinkable aside from inner vision. From the earliest accounts in Genesis to the eschatological scenarios of Revelation, the intuitive is indispensable to comprehending the message and hearing the Word.

Listening Prayerfully. The practice of reading, thinking, and praying Scripture is ancient in Christian tradition and goes back in part to the monastic practice called *lectio divina.* Basil Pennington describes it as a passive approach to Scripture, aimed less at the assimilation of information than at the opening of oneself to the Word, or as Bernard of Clairvaux expressed it, preparing oneself for "visits of the Word."[28] It provides a way of listening, consonant with Jung's view of Scripture as a soul book.

Since conscious technique is the better part of good habit, many programs for "praying the Scriptures" have been proposed.[29] The basic format consists of three steps: 1. reading a chapter, a few paragraphs, or even a few verses; 2. marking those words, phrases, or images that speak with special meaning, and reflecting on them one by one; 3. praying or "conversing with God" over several of these. George Martin describes his technique in *Reading Scripture as the Word of God:*

> When I have finished my set reading, I turn to prayer and go back over the verses I've marked, one by one, using them as material for reflection. I listen to what the Lord may wish to say to me through them, making them the basis of my prayer. My experience is that

there is usually something, even in the driest passages of Scripture, that will strike my mind in a fresh way and provide food for prayer. If one marked passage doesn't provide enough basis for prayer, I turn to another one. Sometimes, though, the first passage provides ample material for my prayer time, as I trace and retrace its message and implication for me.[30]

Prayer is an act of the soul in focus, and when trained on Scripture provides one of the best ways to hear its Word and to be drawn into the presence of the One who speaks.

Active Imagination and the Art of Proclaiming Scripture

Jung's method of active imagination teaches us that the interpretation of the biblical text is possible in more than one mode. The rabbis were among the first to demonstrate this fact. For them Scripture was a many-faceted jewel. When they held it up to the light, viewing it from various angles, it would radiate new hues and glisten in unsuspecting colors. Some of the light would illumine the conscience, some the soul and its aspiration, some the everyday problems of the individual and community, and some would supply insight into the origin and destiny of the human journey. One of their approaches they called *peshat*, "to make plain," focusing on the literal meaning of Scripture. A second approach was called *remez* or "hint," seeking out the allegorical or typological meanings that pointed to the processual and personal parallels between the biblical story and their story. A third approach, most widely used, was *derash* or "search" (whence Midrash), using Hillel's seven interpretive rules or *middoth* to make orderly inferences from the law to life. A fourth method called *sod* or "secret" searched out the sacred mysteries.

It was out of such insights that Christian scholars during the first sixteen centuries—Origen, Clement, Jerome, Augustine, Albertus Magnus, Thomas Aquinas, and Martin Luther among them—practiced a four-fold method of scriptural interpretation: the literal, the allegorical, the moral, and the anagogical. A Latin quatrain summarized their functions:

> Litera gesta docet;
> Quid credas allegoria;

Moralis quid agis;
Quo tendas anagogia.

In translation it read:

The literal (reading) teaches us the past,
The allegorical, what we believe;
The moral, what we must do;
The anagogical, what we must aspire to.

One of the great tragedies of the medieval period is that the allegorical method was misused. It was enlisted by the church to justify metaphysical teachings, political theories, and social doctrines that had nothing to do with Scripture. The resulting suspicion led to a growing preference for the literal approach and the elimination of all the rest. The ban on *allegoria, moralis,* and *anagogia* has lasted well into the twentieth century, especially among biblical scholars.

We have reached a point, however, with the help of Jung and others, of recognizing, even in biblical critical circles,[31] that a strictly literal approach to the text will not suffice. The biblical authors knew this long ago,[32] and tradition has recognized it ever since. It has assigned, on the one hand, biblical scholars to do the work of the literal interpretation of the text; but on the other, it has assigned makers of sermons, of Bible stories, of miracle plays, liturgies, cantatas, stained glass windows, paintings and statues to do the work of allegorizing, moralizing, and uplifting. All have demonstrated beyond any question of legitimacy that much more is to be seen, felt, sensed, and intuited in Scripture than what a literal reading alone can render.

The wisdom of the church—and of biblical scholarship—rests in the long run on its ability to deploy all its faculties in the task of interpreting Scripture. It must begin with the deployment of a battalion of scholars and thinkers to bring up the siege works of scholarly criticism to wrestle with Scripture until it yields some of the historical secrets so precious to anyone who loves the text. But it must also deploy moral theologians, preachers, and prophets to awaken the conscience and demonstrate how the moral passion of Scripture can be translated into moral action today. It must also deploy its painters, sculptors, liturgists, composers, and writers of psalms to interrupt our dark moods with the glories of their art, seducing our senses with their truths even when our minds seem dulled. And it must deploy its spiritual directors, counselors, pastors, and a vast army of unsung saints to teach us to read Scripture, to listen for its Word, and to pray its truth into our lives.

Letting Go with Scripture

It is probably a true story. It tells of an eloquent and powerful black preacher in the deep South who was asked how he prepared his sermons. He responded: "First, I read myself full; then I think myself clear; I pray myself humble, and I let myself go."

No words capture more faithfully the task and sequence of scriptural interpretation. Having done the necessary homework of reading, thinking, and prayer, the scriptural interpreter is asked to go one step further of "letting go." As professionals in any field will attest, the culminating act of "letting go" can be exhilarating and in itself educational. It requires daring, a sense of freedom, and a certain self-confidence. It brings with it the thrill and threat of performance, born of the conviction that the text must be "performed"—that is, followed through, carried out. When we have executed this archetypal task, we dare not succumb, as Jung warns, to the illusion that we have exhausted the topic or spoken the last word. Our efforts are at best reasonably successful attempts at translating the Word into the special metaphor inspired by our training, experience, insight, study, and prayer. But it is a task to be done and it belongs to the scriptural interpreter who, from Jung's perspective, must dare to dream the Word onward and so hopefully advance its work of bringing souls into God-consciousness. As the Psalmist expresses it:

> Let this be recorded for a generation to come,
> so that a people yet unborn may praise the LORD. (Ps. 102:18)

CHAPTER VII

God, the Bible, and the Self in Jungian Perspective

> He had taken the Bible's commandments as his guide; he believed in God as the Bible prescribed and as his forefathers had taught him. But he did not know the immediate living God who stands, omnipotent and free, above His Bible and His Church, who calls upon man to partake of His freedom.
>
> —*Memories, Dreams, Reflections*[1]

> I find that all my thoughts circle around God like the planets around the sun, and are as irresistibly attracted by Him.
>
> —*Memories, Dreams, Reflections*[2]

> The Christian puts his Church and his Bible between himself and his unconscious.
>
> —*Man and His Symbols*[3]

Chinese specialist Erwin Rousselle tells of a course he took with a Taoist secret society master. When the course was completed, the master presented each of his students with a farewell gift. To the Chinese students he gave a Chinese book, but to Rousselle, a European, he gave a copy of the Bible.[4] With this gesture, the Taoist master acknowledged the fact of the longstanding affair between Scripture and the Western psyche. But he also expressed the judgment, with which Jung would concur, that the Bible is better equipped than any religious text from the East to nourish the soul of a person with spiritual and cultural roots in the West. Jung found this true in his personal life. As attracted as he was to the religious texts and theosophy of the East, he nevertheless found himself drawn to Scripture, to its words and symbols, its archetypal figures and stories, to nourish and sustain his own inner life.[5]

Despite this deep appreciation of Scripture, however, Jung was not blind to the fact that the Bible can be a bane as well as a blessing for Western society, depending on how it is understood and used. Jung expressed this notion in his last major essay, "Approaching the Unconscious," completed in 1961. It is a statement worth pondering for anyone who loves Scripture, and it serves as a keynote for what Jung has to say about the relationship of those three great realities in his life—God, the Bible, and the Self.

Jung writes that "the Christian puts his Church and his Bible between himself and his unconscious."[6] In context, this should not be read as an absolute statement, true of all Christians everywhere, but rather as a description that in Jung's judgment Christians too often forestall their own experience of God in deference to what others tell them about him. We might rephrase this statement to read: "Too often Christians allow their church or their Bible to stand between themselves and their experience of the holy." Jung is not disparaging church or Bible. He regards both as indispensable and inevitable testimony to revelatory events. What he is affirming is that, when wrongly conceived, both church and Scripture can discourage rather than encourage the experience of the holy. When wrongly construed, they can obstruct rather than assist in the disclosure of what God might be revealing within the depth of individual souls for our own time and place.

Historical Protestantism, of course, will agree with at least half of what Jung says, namely that the church can at times stand between oneself and the experience of the holy. Luther, Calvin, Huss, and a host of others have voiced the judgment that on certain issues they preferred the light of their own conscience to that of the official church. The prophets also were convinced out of their own personal experience that justice and righteousness were dearer to the divine than the sacrifice and song proferred by official religion. The notion of institutional religion obstructing God's truth as revealed to his prophets and saints is not foreign to the Protestant mentality.

But what of the Bible? Can it, too, stand between believers and their experience of the holy? Jung would say "yes." Some post-Reformation Roman Catholic theologians along with many contemporary Protestants would agree, citing any number of Bible-centered individuals and groups so preoccupied with Scripture that they are blind and deaf to all the times and places in which God may be speaking in our own times, whether in liturgies, traditions, conciliar decrees, and dogmas, or in the lives of saints, ancient and modern, or in the depths of individual souls. The Bible too, Jung maintains, can obstruct the experience of the holy, depending on how it is conceived and used by its readers.

The Uses (and Misuses) of Scripture

A graduate student of mine once gave a class report in which he mused on all the different ways the Bible is used in our culture. In the first place, he said, with tongue in cheek, the Bible can be used as a paperweight or doorstop. These are not the most common uses of Scripture, but no doubt are real ones.

More seriously, he noted that the Bible can be used by college students to pass an examination in a course on *The Bible,* cramming on Bible facts the night before the exam. The Bible can also be used as a research tool by the biblical scholar to trace ancient social customs, habits, and laws of the past. Or the Bible can be used just to pass the time away, as in a motel room, when one reaches into the drawer to leaf through the Gideon Bible.

The Bible can also be used by a preacher to find a text for a sermon, as a kind of Bartlett's Book of Quotations for the pulpit. It can also be used as a symbol in the home, on a bookshelf or coffee table, saying to visitors that "this is a home where the Bible is respected," though one recalls Samuel Sandmel's reminder that "more people praise the Bible than read it, more read it than understand it; and more understand it than conscientiously follow it."[7] The Bible can also be used by non-Christians to find out what Christianity is about. Richard Rubenstein, a Jewish scholar, tells us how as a youngster he had wanted to read the New Testament to find out who Jesus was and what his Christian neighbors believed.

More seriously, the Bible can be used as a proof-text to support a particular dogma or theological point. We are all familiar with this use, which is sometimes found on central theological issues but more often than not on religio-political types of questions having to do with evolution, or whether God wants women to be ordained, or whether homosexuals should be excluded from church fellowship. Finally, and as a related point, the Bible can be used as a tool of the shadow side of individuals and religious institutions, to defend tyrannies, to justify atrocities, and to warrant social, religious, and racial suppressions of the worst sort. As Jung comments, the religion of love is known to have assisted at the greatest blood baths in the world's history.[8]

Some of these uses of Scripture are, of course, legitimate. But none come up to its primary function, which in Jung's judgment is not to provide historical data for scholars, nor texts for preachers, nor proof-texts for theologians, nor programs for tyrants. The Bible has a higher calling—to awaken the soul to an awareness of the holy.

Karl Barth once offered an image that expresses this well. He compares the Bible reader to a man standing at a third or fourth floor window of an apartment building and looking down at the sidewalk below, where he sees a group of people standing, talking excitedly to one another, and pointing to something in the sky above the roof of the building, over the man's head and out of his line of vision. Barth compares the people on the street to the biblical writers and their inspired reports about God. The man at the window is the modern biblical reader. His interest is not just to stand up there, watching the crowd, straining to hear what they say. His goal is to run down the stairs *to see for himself.*

The purpose of Scripture is not just to issue a series of reports about God's past action which we can accept by hearsay. It is to invite and excite the readers to look with their own eyes and listen with their own ears to the One to whom the Bible with all its images, stories, and metaphors unerringly points. It is not the God of the past, but the Living God of the past, present, and future who continues to act, to speak, and to express his will—in church, in Scripture, but also in the depth of the human soul.

The Problem of G-O-D

We are moving back into a period when we can use God-language again. During the "death of God" period there was a profound reluctance to use the three-letter word *G-O-D* to refer to the holy because it, like any other word, somehow seemed so inadequate to the reality to which it referred. In fact, many of us still have those feelings, suspecting that the orthodox Jew in refusing to repeat the name of the Lord may be the wisest of all, in the conviction that no human can speak the name that does justice to the reality and fullness of the holy.

In conventional Christian use the word *God* has commonly referred either to God the creator, God the Father of our Lord Jesus Christ, or God whose spirit breathes through the pages of Scripture and in the lives of righteous souls. But when we take a tour into the back roads of human experience, especially in places where suffering and tragedy have struck, we find the name *God* used in other ways and in different tones. There we can hear God spoken of as the one who "allowed my grandson to die," or allowed devastation to be visited on our city, or the One who permitted a night of terror to descend upon thousands of innocent victims in the Holocaust.

The word *God* is not "kid's stuff"; it is not the simple, uncomplicated, settled term we sometimes think but carries within its depth mysteries, paradoxes, and hard truths that shake the soul. John F. Kennedy used to say that there were three great realities: God, human folly, and humor. "Since the first two are beyond our comprehension," he would add, "we will have to do what we can with the third." Jung's understanding of God shares this sense of mystery, and he spells out his understanding of God from two perspectives he identifies as those of "personality No. 1" and of "personality No. 2."

Personality No. 1 and Personality No. 2

Jung tells us that from childhood he recognized he was like "two persons" with two different ways of experiencing himself and his world. On the one hand he saw himself from a "public" perspective, as "the son of my parents who went to school, and was less intelligent, attentive, hard-working, decent, and clean than other boys,"[9] but who later became an excellent student, was admitted to the university, and in time became identified professionally with certain achievements in the field of psychology. He called this self "personality No. 1," the objective, visible, external self known by parents, teachers, relatives, friends, peers, and recognized by himself as his public image.

But he had another side. This second side was "grown-up—old, in fact—skeptical, mistrustful, remote from the world of people, but close to nature, the earth, the sun, the moon, the weather, all living creatures, and above all close to the night, to dreams, and to whatever 'God' worked directly in him."[10] Jung tells us he put the name of God in quotation marks here because God at times seemed to him to be closer to nature than to people. "It seemed to me," he writes, "that the high mountains, the rivers, lakes, trees, flowers, and animals far better exemplified the essence of God than men with their ridiculous clothes, their meanness, vanity, mendacity, and abhorrent egotism— all qualities with which I was only too familiar from myself, that is, from personality No. 1, the schoolboy of 1890."[11]

The two often seemed to be in conflict. He recalls between his sixteenth and nineteenth years how personality No. 1 became more and more prominent in his life. The more he focused on objective interests—zoology, paleontology, geology, archeology, and Greco-Roman and Egyptian history—the more personality No. 2 became "doubtful and distasteful" to him. Personality No. 1 had important things to do; it wanted to be up and about, impatient with the passivity and contemplativeness of personality No. 2.

When Jung was at school in the presence of his friends he could forget about personality No. 2. But when he was by himself, at home or out in the country, personality No. 1 with its "worries about the choice of a profession sank below the horizon,"[12] and personality No. 2 would return, reminding him that, beside the world of public facts and projects, there "existed another realm, like a temple in which anyone who entered was transformed and suddenly overpowered by a vision of the whole cosmos, so that he could only marvel and admire, forgetful of himself."[13]

These two personalities, one objective, public, professional, active, and largely rational, and the other, subjective, personal, somewhat passive and intuitive, coexisted in Jung throughout his life. In Jung's mature adult life the one represented Jung the psychologist, scientist, and clinical student of the human psyche; the other represented Jung the individual person immersed in the stream of life, working out a story whose beginning and end were a mystery, and living out of a destiny he felt prescribed for him. Jung writes his thoughts about God speaking from both modes.

God in Jung's Professional Psychological Perspective

Jung's point-of-view as a professional psychologist is documented in the eighteen volumes of his *Collected Works*. Here he writes as an empiricist, objectively studying the range of phenomena associated with the human personality, including religion: religious ritual and symbolism, religious experience, and above all God-language and God-images that appear in every culture.

As noted earlier, Jung undertook research on religious phenomena against Freud's wishes. Freud had warned him against the "black tide of mud of occultism," which Jung took to include "virtually everything that philosophy and religion . . . had learned about the psyche."[14] Over against Freud, Jung maintained that religion is "incontestably one of the earliest and most universal expressions of the human mind," and that "any psychology which touches upon the psychological structure of human personality cannot avoid taking note of the fact that religion isn't only a sociological and historical phenomenon, but also something of considerable personal concern to a great number of individuals."[15] The result was the break with Freud in 1913, just seven years after their first meeting.

This is not to say that Jung thought of himself as a theologian. Jung takes pains to distinguish the theologian's task from that of the psychologist. The role of the theologian is to talk about God, but the task of the psychologist is to talk about religious experience and the God-images used to express it. The theologian, Jungs says "puts the accent on the 'imprinter,' but the psychologist emphasizes the 'imprint.' " A basic observation Jung makes about the "imprint" or God-image is that it is not something invented, but rather an "expression that comes upon man spontaneously."[16] It is not produced rationally or consciously, but rather comes to us, without prompting, from a realm of the psyche far removed from all human volition. God-images are irrepressible and they are universal.

From this psychic "fact" Jung draws the fundamental conclusion that the human psyche is "natively religious" (*naturaliter religiosa*),[17] that the "religious impulse rests on an instinctive basis and is therefore a specifically human function."[18] This does not mean that the religious impulse cannot be suppressed, but rather that it will keep coming back no matter how much one might wish to rule it out. Jung tells the story of an articulate young Jewish woman who had come to him beset by attacks of deep anxiety. In the course of the first meeting he inquired about relationships within her family. When he asked about her grandfather, the girl closed her eyes. Jung observed, "I realized at once that here lay the heart of the problem." On further inquiry Jung learned her grandfather had been a Hasidic rabbi. She referred to him as a "kind of saint" who "also possessed second sight. But that is all nonsense," she added. In her total rejection of this part of her past, Jung observes, the girl had cut herself off from those "mythological and religious ideas" she needed in order to express her deep spiritual nature, which she had suppressed for years behind a life dedicated exclusively to the development of her intellect and her public image.[19] "When life runs smoothly without religion, the loss remains as good as unnoticed," Jung writes. "But when suffering comes, it is another matter. That is when people begin to seek a way out and reflect about the meaning of life and its bewildering and painful experience."[20] Jung found that such a rediscovery frequently occurs in the second half of life. Jung observed that "among all my patients in the second half of life—that is to say, over thirty-five—there has not been one whose problem in the last resort was not that of finding a religious outlook on life. It is safe to say," he adds, "that every one of them fell ill because he had lost that which the living religions of every age have given to their fellows, and none of them has been really healed who did not regain his religious outlook."[21] Jung likes to quote the medieval Latin quip, "*Naturam expellas furca, tamen atque recurret*"— "You can drive nature out with a pitchfork, but it always comes back." So, too, with religion. It is an irrepressible part of human nature and is always waiting at the door.

What does Jung mean by "religion"? "I want to make clear that by the term 'religion,' I do not mean a creed. . . . We might say . . . that the term designates the attitude peculiar to a consciousness which has been changed by the experience of the *numinosum*."[22] Religion is not at root a matter of creeds and concepts, but of experience. One of the problems Jung found with much of Western religion in his time is that it is too full of concepts. One doesn't have any obligation to a concept. By stressing external religious beliefs, "Christian civilization has proved hollow to a terrifying degree: it is all veneer, but the inner man has remained untouched and therefore unchanged. His soul is out of key with his external beliefs. . . ."[23] For this reason, Jung infers, many Westerners have turned to the religions of the East, attracted by its emphasis on meditation, spiritual discipline, and experiential religion. Jung appreciates Eastern spirituality, but believes the West must develop its own. "Do not imitate," he advises. "Study yoga, but above all find out who it is using the yoga."[24] "The West will produce its own yoga in the course of centuries and it will be created on the basis of Christianity."[25]

What role does religion, as Jung understands it from the perspective of a professional psychologist, play in the life of the psyche? First, religion provides a system of symbols, stories, and myths that enables the self to objectify those inner truths and processes that defy scientific observation—sin and forgiveness, spiritual healing and rebirth, the old and new person, questions of whence we have come and whither we are going. Second, religion provides a counterbalance to mass-mindedness, a point Jung makes emphatically in his book, *The Undiscovered Self*.[26] In it he invites the individual to resist the psychopathology of the mass, and its desire for power, and to call for a new way. Third, religion has as one of its primary aims the care and healing of souls. "Religions are psychotherapeutic systems in the truest sense of the word. . . . They express the whole range of the psychic problem in powerful images; they are the avowal and recognition of the soul, and at the same time the revelation of the soul's nature."[27]

At the end of his Terry Lectures, Jung made this summarizing statement on the role of religion in the life of the psyche as he sees it from the standpoint of a professional psychologist:

> Religious experience is absolute. It cannot be disputed. . . . No matter what the world thinks about religious experience, the one who has it possesses a great treasure, a thing that has become for him a source of life, meaning and beauty, and that has given a new splendor to the

world and to mankind. He has *pistis* [faith] and peace. Where is the criterion by which you could say that such a life is not legitimate, that such an experience is not valid and that such *pistis* is mere illusion? Is there, as a matter of fact, any better truth about the ultimate things than the one that helps you to live? . . . The thing that cures a neurosis must be as convincing as the neurosis, and since the latter is only too real, the helpful experience must be equally real. . . . Nobody can know what the ultimate things are. We must, therefore, take them as we experience them. And if such experience helps to make your life healthier, more beautiful, more complete, and more satisfactory to yourself and to those you love, you may safely say: "This was the grace of God."[28]

God in Jung's Personal Perspective

In a BBC television interview on "Face to Face," made two years before his death, Jung was asked by interviewer John Freeman, "Do you believe in God?" Jung replied that he did not *believe* anything; either he *knew* something or he didn't. He went on to say, "I do not need to believe in God; I *know*."[29]

Unable to answer all the letters this comment precipitated, Jung published his response in a letter to *The Listener,* January 21, 1960:

My opinion about "knowledge of God" is an unconventional way of thinking and I quite understand if it should be suggested that I am no Christian. Yet I think of myself as a Christian since I am entirely based upon Christian concepts. I only try to escape their internal contradictions by introducing a more modest attitude, which takes into consideration the immense darkness of the human mind. . . . I did not say in the broadcast, "There is a God." I said, "I do not need to believe in God; I *know*." Which does not mean: I do know a certain God . . . but rather: I do know that I am obviously confronted with a factor unknown in itself, which I call "God." . . . I remember Him, I evoke Him, whenever I use His name overcome by anger or by fear, whenever I involuntarily say, "Oh God." . . . Since I *know* of my collision with a superior will in my own psychical system, *I know of God,* and if I should venture the illegitimate hypostasis of my image, I would say, of *a God beyond good and evil,* just as much dwelling in myself as everywhere else: *Deus est circulus cuius centrum est ubique, cuius circumferentia vero nusquam* [God is the circle whose center is everywhere, and whose circumference truly is nowhere]."[30]

The bulk of Jung's personal statements about God, published posthumously in his autobiography, *Memories, Dreams, Reflections,* and in the two volumes of his letters, *C.G. Jung Letters,* [31] follow this same line. God is one who is known, not just believed in.

This contention stood at the heart of Jung's dispute with his pastor father, who had repeatedly admonished, "You always want to think; one ought not to think but believe." But Jung had responded within himself silently, "No, one must experience and know." [32] His father's religion of sheer belief seemed "stale and hollow," strong on concepts, but weak on experience. His father's sermons, rooted in what Jung called "theological religion," often sounded to Jung "like a tale told by someone who knows it only by hearsay and cannot quite believe it himself." [33]

Jung recalls how he had looked forward to the explanation of the great mystery of the Trinity when taking catechism with his father. But, Jung reports: "When we got that far, my father said, 'We now come to the Trinity, but we'll skip that, for I really understand nothing of it myself.' " Jung comments, "I admired my father's honesty, but on the other hand I was profoundly disappointed . . . they know nothing about it and don't give it a thought." [34]

Jung at one point turned to theological texts to see what they had to say about evil. Jung had seen what he took to be evil. He had witnessed drownings in the Rhine. He had seen "diseased and dying fishes . . . mangy foxes . . . frozen or starved birds . . . pitiless tragedies concealed in a flowery meadow: earthworms tormented to death by ants, insects that tore each other apart piece by piece, and so on." [35] In his search for an answer, he found that the theological writings either said nothing, or, after a long technical discussion, concluded that "the origin of evil was 'unexplained and inexplicable,' " which to Jung said that they simply did not want to think about it. [36]

An event that confirmed Jung's suspicion of the hollowness of "theological religion" was the experience of his first communion. He had been led to believe it would be a culminating experience. But once into the service he noted that it seemed to look like any other service. "All were stiff, solemn, and it seemed to me, uninterested. I looked on in suspense, but could not see or guess whether anything unusual was going on inside the old men. . . . I saw no sadness and no joy." All he could think when he received the elements was that the bread tasted flat and the little sip of wine tasted sour. "Then came the final prayer, and the people went out, neither depressed nor illumined with joy, but with faces that said, 'So that's that.' " Jung writes:

> I had reached the pinnacle of religious initiation, had expected something—I know not what—to happen, and nothing at all had happened. . . . This was called the "Christian religion," but none of it had anything to do with God as I had experienced Him. On the other hand it was quite clear that Jesus, the man, did have to do with God; he had despaired in Gethsemane and on the cross, after having taught that God was a kind and loving father. He too, then, must have seen the fearfulness of God. That I could understand, but what was the purpose of this wretched memorial service with the flat bread and the sour wine? . . . "Why, that is not religion at all," I thought. "It is an absence of God."[37]

Jung writes that at this point he "was seized with the most vehement pity for my father. All at once I understood the tragedy of his profession and his life."[38] This insight was confirmed years later when his father hinted of his religious doubts and exhorted Jung to "be anything you like except a theologian."[39] What was amiss in his father's faith? Jung writes, "He had taken the Bible's commandments as his guide; he believed in God as the Bible prescribed and as his forefathers had taught him. But he did not know the immediate living God who stands omnipotent and free, above His Bible and His Church, who calls upon man to partake of His freedom."[40]

Who is this immediate, living God of whom Jung speaks and what is his nature? For Jung, God was at the center of all his thinking. In a letter to a clergyman in 1952, Jung writes, "I find that all my thoughts circle around God like the planets around the sun, and are irresistibly attracted by Him. I would feel it to be the grossest sin if I were to oppose any resistance to this force."[41] God for Jung was the "most immediate" and "most evident of all experiences."[42]

Jung acknowledged that all our descriptions of God are limited to the structures of human imagination. "We can imagine God as an eternally flowing current of vital energy that endlessly changes shapes just as easily as we can imagine him as an eternally unmoved unchangeable essence."[43] But all of our God images, whether drawn from nature, philosophy, physics, or anthropology, are the products of the limited human mind, created "in order to express an unfathomable and ineffable experience. The experience alone is real, not to be disputed; but the image can be soiled or broken to pieces. Names and words," Jung writes, "are sorry husks, yet they indicate the quality of what we have experienced."[44]

God as all in all for Jung incorporates the polarities of existence. For Jung, God is light, but he can also be seen as the "darkest, nethermost cause of Nature's blackest deeps."[45] He is the One who is present at creation, but also at the cross, "an annihilating fire and indescribable grace."[46] Scripture echoes this report, on the one hand declaring God's glory and goodness, but on the other speaking of him as the one who "brings darkness" (Jer. 13:16), who is "a consuming fire" (Heb. 12:29), who makes woe as well as weal (Isa. 45:7). Jung frequently cites the formulation of the second-century Pseudo-Clementine Homilies that "God rules the world with a right and a left hand, the right being Christ, the left Satan."[47] For Jung, God is the *mysterium tremendum,* whose will and word, whose plans and purposes transcend human judgment. Shortly before his death, Jung wrote, "To this day God is the name by which I designate all things which cross my wilful path violently and recklessly, all things which upset my subjective views, plans, and intentions and change the course of my life for better or worse."[48]

Jung used the phrase "God's world" to refer to another significant dimension of his experience—the numinous reaches of nature that spoke to him of God. It was the world known so well by personality No. 2, close to earth, sun, and moon. It was not found in the bustle of Basel's city life but away "among rivers and woods, among men and animals in a small village bathed in sunlight, with the winds and the clouds moving over it, and encompassed by dark night in which uncertain things happen. It was no mere locality on the map, but 'God's world,' so ordered by Him and filled with secret meaning . . . a unified cosmos . . . in an eternity where everything is already born and everything has already died."[49]

"God's world" was one to whom Jung's father had introduced him. He had taken his son on a steamship trip from Lucerne to the small village of Vitznau, where a cogwheel railway could be taken to the summit of the Rigi, a high mountain. His father had pressed a ticket into his hand, telling him, "You can ride up to the peak alone. I'll stay here, it's too expensive for the two of us. Be careful not to fall down anywhere." Jung was "speechless with joy." From the peak as he looked into the "unimaginable distances," he thought, "Yes, this is it, my world, the real world . . . where there are no teachers, no schools, no unanswerable questions, where one can *be* without having to ask anything." It was a place of tremendous precipices. "It was all very solemn, and I felt one had to be polite and silent up here for one was in God's world. . . . This was the most precious gift my father had ever given me. For many decades," Jung writes, "this image rose up whenever I was wearied from overwork and sought a point of rest."[50]

Jung admitted that, to some, the expression "God's world" might sound sentimental. But for him it did not have this character at all. "To 'God's world' belongs everything superhuman—dazzling light, the darkness of the abyss, the cold impassivity of infinite space and time, and the uncanny grotesqueness of the irrational world of God. 'God,' for me, was everything."[51]

God is also *within.* Jung makes this point repeatedly. "It would be blasphemy to assert that God can manifest himself everywhere save only in the human soul. Indeed, the very intimacy of the relationship between God and the soul automatically precludes any devaluation of the latter. It would be going perhaps too far to speak of an affinity; but at all events the soul must contain in itself the faculty of relation to God, i.e., a correspondence, otherwise a connection could never come about."[52] It is out of the soul that God-images, moral insight, conscience, theological truth, religious art, liturgy, and prayer emerge. For Jung the psyche or soul is the meeting place between God and humanity.[53] "It is therefore quite unthinkable psychologically for God to be simply the 'wholly other,' for a 'wholly other' could never be one of the soul's deepest and closest intimates—which is precisely what God is."[54]

Scripture, of course, also speaks of the *God within.* Jeremiah tells of the law written upon the heart (Jer. 31:33). Paul appeals to his Corinthian readers as temples of God in whom God's spirit dwells (1 Cor. 3:16). Luke speaks of the kingdom within (Luke 17:21). The author of Deuteronomy tells us that the commandment of the Lord is not too hard for us nor is it far off, neither in heaven nor beyond the sea, "but the word is very near you; it is in your mouth and in your heart, so that you can do it" (Deut. 30:11–14).

Above all, Jung turns to the medieval mystics for insights into the *God within*. Meister Eckhardt, the thirteenth-century father of German mysticism, writes that "he . . . for whom God is not an inward possession, but who must fetch all God for himself from outside in this thing or in that . . . such a man has him not."[55] In poetic form reminiscent of certain nineteenth and twentieth-century church hymns, Angelus Silenius writes:

> In me God is a fire
> And I in Him its glow;
> In common is our life,
> Apart we cannot grow.
> . . . .
> I am the vine, which He
> Doth plant and cherish most;
> The fruit which grows from me
> Is God, the Holy Ghost.[56]

Even St. Augustine, writing in the fourth century, joins in the chorus with his observation: "The life of the body is the soul, but the life of the soul is God."[57]

God is the alpha and omega for Jung, the beginning and end, whose vast world and revelations were as real to Jung as anything could be. "From the beginning," he writes,

> I had a sense of destiny, as though my life was assigned to me by fate and had to be fulfilled. This gave me an inner security, and, though I could never prove it to myself, it proved itself to me. *I* did not have this certainty, *it* had me. Nobody could rob me of the conviction that it was enjoined upon me to do what God wanted and not what I wanted. That gave me the strength to go my own way. Often I had the feeling that in all decisive matters I was no longer among men, but was alone with God. And when I was "there," where I was no longer alone, I was outside time; I belonged to the centuries; and He who then gave answer was He who had always been, who had been before my birth. He who always is was there. These talks with the "Other" were my profoundest experiences: on the one hand a bloody struggle, on the other supreme ecstasy.[58]

Vocatus Atque Non Vocatus, Deus Aderit

For Jung the goal of Scripture is not just to describe God, to tell about his past great deeds, to define his nature, or to quote his words verbatim. Its purpose is to point to the One who is at the center of all being, the "circle whose center is everywhere but whose circumference is unlimited." The function of Scripture for Jung is to tutor the soul in God-consciousness and to bring its readers into the presence of the holy.

This theme resounds throughout Jung's personal and professional life. On his bookplate, on his gravestone, and on the doorway over his house in Küsnacht is this single inscription: *"Vocatus atque non vocatus, Deus aderit"*— "Summoned or not summoned God will be present." In a letter dated November 19, 1960, explaining this inscription over his doorway, Jung writes: "I have put the inscription there to remind my patients and myself: *timor dei initium sapientiae* (the fear of God is the beginning of wisdom). Here another not less important road begins, not the approach to Christianity, but to God himself and this seems to be the ultimate question."[59]

EPILOGUE

Psychological Criticism
and Scriptural Studies

Man's task . . . is to create more and more consciousness.
Memories, Dreams, Reflections[1]

The work of applying psychological and psychoanalytic insight to the reading and interpretation of Scripture is far from a developed art. Yet it seems inevitable and necessary, as an increasing number of biblical scholars would agree,[2] that a *psychological criticism* will emerge in the years ahead as another of the critical tools biblical interpreters can employ in plumbing the depths of Scripture and exploring the role it plays in human consciousness.

The purpose of this volume has been to suggest the contribution Carl Jung's life and work make toward the development of such a *psychological criticism*. Though Jung acknowledges that "psychology has only a modest contribution to make toward a deeper understanding of the phenomena of life and is no nearer than its sister science to absolute knowledge,"[3] at the same time he would insist that the contribution psychology can make is real and significant. It may therefore be well to summarize, as an agenda for future research, what the nature of that contribution in part might be.

The primary contribution Jungian thought would make toward a *psychological criticism* of Scripture would lie in its insistence on the recognition of the reality of the psyche and of the unconscious as a function, not only of the biblical authors, but of biblical readers and interpreters as well. Though it is not yet clear methodologically how this recognition can be applied to the interpretation of specific texts, it is clear that such a recognition sensitizes us to the fact that Scripture is to be studied not only as the product of a historical, literary, sociological, and linguistic process, but also as the product of a psychic process in which the psyche and the unconscious of the author, his community, and the reader and his community all play a role.

A second contribution is the recognition that a text can be an expression and bearer of meanings that reside, as F. C. Grant observes, at "levels below the historical, actual, verbal statement or narrative."[4] A *psychological criticism* would add its voice to that of linguists and philosophers who point to the text as a bearer of symbols, laden with polyvalent meaning, capable of awakening the reader's consciousness, catalyzing the reader's energies, and vitalizing the reader's will.

Third, a *psychological criticism* would take note of the fact that many scriptural motifs and symbols appear to be archetypal in character. They appear "so frequently in widely scattered mythic traditions," Walter Wink comments, that we are justified in regarding them "as a standard component in spiritual development. The very pervasiveness of such stories . . . is evidence that we are dealing with something fundamental to the spiritual journey itself, and not merely with etiological legends invented to 'explain' the origin of things."[5] If this is in fact the case, then one of the concrete goals of a *psychological criticism* will be to amplify the already rich collection of comparative archaeological, historical, and linguistic data gathered by biblical scholars, with the comparative mythological and symbolic data gathered by historians and phenomenologists of religion, in an attempt to perceive as thoroughly as possible the range of values a given biblical symbol or motif can register in the human psyche. As John Dominic Crossan comments, "The full study of a biblical text, either by the same or different scholars, will demand in the future as much use, for example, of James Pritchard's magisterial *Ancient Near Eastern Texts and Pictures* as of Stith Thompson's equally magisterial *Motif Index of Folk-Literature.*"[6]

A fourth function of *psychological criticism* would lie in the realm of hermeneutics, namely to reclaim and reassess the ancient Hebrew midrashic, patristic, and medieval Christian insight that the intention of the biblical text is not only to convey a literal meaning, but to evoke a moral, spiritual, and transformative meaning in the life of the reader. It will want to explore the suspicion, fostered by literary critics, artists, pastoral ministers and others, that a legitimate hermeneutic can involve not only a literal rendering of the text's meaning, but also a non-literal rendering, for example, in worship, art, teaching, preaching, and styles of moral conduct, as well as through a scriptural scholarship sensitive to the metaphorical and symbolic dimension of the text and equal to the exegetical task of exploring and disclosing this dimension.

A fifth function of *psychological criticism* would be to cast light on the psychological dynamics operative within biblical stories, e.g., the patriarchal sagas, the court history in 2 Samuel, the parables and the life of Jesus. To be sure, this particular function lends itself most easily to the temptation of psychologizing, that is, to reading a story as nothing more than an allegory of a favorite psychological model. Despite this danger, however, it is clear, even in those contemporary biblical studies that tend to import Freudian or Jungian structures haphazardly into the text, that on occasion, out of the depth of the author's acquaintance with the nature of the human psyche, profound suggestions can be made into the dynamics of the story that would seem to open its meaning rather than to submit it to the template of a model foreign to the text.[7]

A sixth function of *psychological criticism* can be to deepen our understanding of certain psychological and spiritual realities fundamental to biblical consciousness, e.g., the experience of sin and grace, of forgiveness and spiritual *enthousiasmos,* the phenomena of conversion and prophetic inspiration. Commenting on the biblical understanding of the experience of "salvation", for example, Robin Scroggs writes, that "salvation means changes, changes in how we think, in how we feel, in how we act. And that means, or so it seems to me, that psychological intuitions and, perhaps, even explicitly psychological models and terminology can give us insight into what these changes are in ourselves and others."[8]

Finally, *psychological criticism* can help us look with greater critical precision at the effect Scripture has had on its readers, individually and corporately, religiously and theologically, socially and institutionally. In his classic 1971 article, "The Study of Religion and the Study of the Bible,"[9] Wilfred Cantwell Smith made the point that a new generation of biblical scholars is needed to study the post-history of Scripture as well as its pre-history, to examine not only what it is that has produced Scripture but what it is that Scripture has produced, to explore biblical effects as well as biblical origins. Such study would entail a closer examination not only of what Scripture brings to the reader, but also what readers bring to Scripture and the effects the text is capable of evoking, both for better and worse in the history of tradition.

In summary, it would be the goal of *psychological criticism* to explore the role of Scripture in the life of the soul. The territory is *terra incognita* in large part, not only because it has been sparsely explored, but because the subject matter is so resistant to precise description. But the reality of the psychic, soulful, spiritual element in the making, transmission, and interpretation of Scripture is nevertheless imposing, and it will be the task of *psychological criticism* to map its reaches more precisely.

Notes

Abbreviations for Standard Works Cited:

CW C. G. Jung, *The Collected Works of C. G. Jung,* ed. Gerhard Adler, Michael Fordham, Sir Herbert Read, and William McGuire; tr. R. F. C. Hull, Bollingen Series XX (Princeton: Princeton University Press, 1953–78), vols. I–XX.

Jacobi Jolande Jacobi, *The Psychology of C. G. Jung,* revised edition (New Haven: Yale University Press, 1971).

Letters C. G. Jung Letters, *I–II,* ed. Gerhard Adler and Aniela Jaffé, Bollingen Series XCV (Princeton: Princeton University Press, 1973–75).

M&S C. G. Jung, Marie-Louise von Franz, Joseph L. Henderson, Jolande Jacobi, and Aniela Jaffé, *Man and His Symbols* (New York: Doubleday & Co., 1971).

MDR C. G. Jung, *Memories, Dreams, Reflections,* ed. Aniela Jaffé; tr. Richard and Clara Winston (New York: Pantheon, 1963).

Preface

1. "Psychological Study of the Bible," in Jacob Neusner, ed., *Religions in Antiquity: Essays in Memory of Erwin Ramsdell Goodenough, Numen,* Spl. XIV (Leiden: Brill, 1969), pp. 112 f.

C. G. Jung Chronology

1. Cf. the extensive chronology in Joseph Campbell, *The Portable Jung* (New York: Viking Press, 1971), pp. xxxiii–xlii; cf. also Gerhard Wehr, *Portrait of Jung, An Illustrated Biography,* tr. W. A. Hargreaves (New York: Herder and Herder, 1971), pp. 168–70.
2. Wehr, op. cit., p. 162.

Chapter I: *"What Has Jung to Do with the Bible?"*

1. *CW* XI, "Answer to Job," p. 363.
2. Wilfred Cantwell Smith, "The Study of Religion and the Study of the Bible," *Journal of the American Academy of Religion*, XXXIX, 1971, pp. 131–40, introduces and develops this distinction.
3. *CW* XI, "Answer to Job," p. 363.
4. *MDR*, p. 42.
5. *CW* XI, "Psychology and Religion," pp. 21–22.
6. *MDR*, p. 87.
7. *Letters, I*, p. 65.
8. Cf. Wehr, op. cit., p. 84; *CW* X, "The Undiscovered Self," p. 276; *MDR*, p. 221; *CW* X, "The Spiritual Problem of Modern Man," p. 88; *CW* XI, "Psychology and Religion," p. 49; *CW* X, "Wotan," p. 186; *CW* IV, "The Father in the Destiny of the Individual," pp. 316f., italics added.
9. *MDR*, p. 181.
10. *Letters, I*, p. 202.
11. *CW* X, "The Meaning of Psychology for Modern Man," p. 152.
12. Morton Kelsey, "A Little Child Shall Lead Them," *The Pecos Benedictine* (Dec. 1976), p. 1; cf. *CW* XVI, "Fundamental Questions of Psychotherapy," p. 121.
13. *MDR*, pp. 37–38.
14. Ibid., p. 88.
15. Laurens van der Post, *Jung and the Story of Our Time* (New York: Vintage Books, 1975), p. 189.
16. Miguel Serrano, *C. G. Jung & Herman Hesse* (New York: Schocken Books, 1966), p. 108.
17. Jung uses the term *numinous* to refer to the spiritual or divine, as a reality that belongs in part to the realm of the unknown.

Chapter II: *Jung's Psychology: An Internal Biographical Account*

1. *MDR*, p. 206.
2. (New York: Harper Colophon Books, 1977), p. xii.
3. Van der Post, op. cit., p. 4.
4. *MDR*, p. 88.
5. Ibid., p. 233.
6. Ibid., p. 93.
7. Ibid., p. 43.
8. Ibid.
9. Ibid., p. 40.
10. Ibid., p. 56.
11. Ibid., pp. 92 f.

12. *CW* XI, "Psychology and Religion," p. 46.
13. *MDR*, p. 75.
14. Van der Post, op. cit., pp. 79f.
15. *MDR*, p. 91.
16. Ibid., p. 60.
17. Jung comments, "In investigating the realm of free creative fantasy we have to rely, more almost than anywhere else, on a broad empiricism; and though this enjoins on us a high degree of modesty with regard to the accuracy of individual results, it by no means obliges us to pass over in silence what has happened and been observed, simply from fear of being execrated as unscientific." *CW* IV, "On the Significance of Number Dreams," p. 53.
18. *MDR*, p. 32.
19. Ibid., pp. 108f.
20. Ibid.
21. Ibid., p. 206.
22. Ibid., p. 127.
23. Ibid., pp. 125 f.
24. Ibid., p. 127.
25. Ibid., pp. 117, 124f.
26. *CW* II, "The Association Method," pp. 439–463, especially p. 440.
27. Ibid., p. 217.
28. *M&S*, p. 40.
29. *MDR*, p. 169.
30. Ibid., pp. 11–12.
31. Ibid., p. 89.
32. *CW* VIII, "General Aspects of Dream Psychology," p. 266.
33. *CW* XVI, "The Practical Use of Dream Analysis," p. 158.
34. Campbell, op. cit., pp. xxii–xxiii.
35. *CW* XI, "Psychology and Religion," pp. 24ff.
36. E. A. Bennet, *What Jung Really Said* (New York: Schocken Books, 1966), p. 114.
37. Cited in Jolande Jacobi, *Complex, Archetype, Symbol in the Psychology of C. G. Jung,* tr. Ralph Manheim, Bollingen Series LVII (Princeton: Princeton University Press, 1959), p. 125.
38. *CW* XVI, "The Practical Use of Dream Analysis," p. 142.
39. *MDR,* pp. 150 f.
40. Ibid., p. 178.
41. Ibid., p. 189.
42. Ibid., p. 192.
43. Ibid., p. 174.
44. Ibid., p. 195.
45. Ibid., p. 192.

46. Ibid., p. 199.
47. Ibid., p. 401; cf. *CW* VIII, p. 185.
48. *CW* III, "Schizophrenia," pp. 261–2.
49. Campbell, op. cit., p. xxxi.
50. *M&S*, p. 67.
51. Campbell, op. cit., p. xiii, quoting Jung.
52. *CW* XI, "Psychology and Religion," p. 104.
53. Tr. S. E. Jellieffe (New York: Dover Publications, 1971). Originally published under the title, *Problems of Mysticism and Its Symbolism* (Eng. tr.).
54. *MDR*, p. 209.
55. *CW* VII, "The Relations Between the Ego and the Unconscious," p. 173.
56. *CW* X, "The Meaning of Psychology for Modern Man," p. 137.
57. *CW* VIII, "On the Nature of Dreams," p. 292.
58. *CW* XI, "Foreword to White's 'God and the Unconscious,' " p. 307.
59. *CW* X, "The Spiritual Problem of Modern Man," p. 86.
60. See Wehr, op. cit., p. 49, n. 50; Bennet, op. cit., p. 172.
61. *CW* VII, "The Relations Between the Ego and the Unconscious," p. 178.
62. Serrano, op. cit., p. 56.
63. *Jacobi*, p. 134, n.3.
64. Wehr, op. cit., p. 156.
65. *MDR*, p. 91.
66. *CW* X, "The Meaning of Psychology for Modern Man," p. 149.
67. *CW* X, "Epilogue to 'Essays on Contemporary Events,' " p. 235.
68. *M&S*, p. 101.
69. *CW* X, "The Undiscovered Self," p. 298.
70. *CW* X, "Epilogue to 'Essays on Contemporary Events,' " p. 228.
71. *CW* X, "The Fight with the Shadow," p. 218.
72. *CW* X, "The Undiscovered Self," p. 276.
73. *CW* X, "After the Catastrophe," p. 217.
74. *M&S*, pp. 101f.
75. *CW* X, "The Undiscovered Self," p. 305.

Chapter III: The Bible and the Life of the Soul

1. *M&S*, p. 102.
2. *CW* XI, "Answer to Job," p. 362.
3. (New York: Scribner's, 1967), pp. 40–41.
4. Hillman, *Insearch*, p. 43.
5. Tr. R. F. C. Hull, Bollingen Series XXI (New York: Pantheon Books, 1950), p. 21.
6. Wehr, op. cit., pp. 153–4, n. 189.
7. *CW* VIII, "On Psychic Energy," p. 8.

8. *CW* X, "The Spiritual Problem of Modern Man," p. 90.
9. *CW* XII, "Introduction to the Religious and Psychological Problems of Alchemy," pp. 12–13.
10. *CW* IV, "On Kranefeldt's 'Secret Ways of the Mind,' " p. 332.
11. *CW* XI, "Psychology and Religion," p. 84.
12. *CW* X, "The Undiscovered Self," p. 269.
13. *MDR*, p. 216.
14. *CW* XI, "Answer to Job," p. 363.
15. Ibid., pp. 360–62.
16. Ibid., p. 359.
17. Ibid., p. 360.
18. Ibid., p. 464.
19. This particular insight represents only one of several dimensions of Jung's understanding of the psychological and historical significance of the Dogma of the Assumption. Cf. *CW* XI, "Answer to Job," pp. 461–9.
20. Ibid., p. 452.
21. Ibid., p. 467.
22. Cited in Morris Philipson, *Outline of a Jungian Aesthetics* (Evanston, IL: Northwestern University Press, 1963), p. 128.
23. Ibid., pp. 125f.
24. See Jung's comment on the Christ-figure as the exemplification of the archetype of the self in chapter V; also *CW* XI, "Answer to Job," p. 441.
25. *Answer to Job* concerns itself with two such "truths from the unconscious" that wait to be realized in modern consciousness. Both truths are voiced in Scripture. The first has to do with the reality of evil in "God's world." The second deals with the conceptualization of God as being present in human beings, in human flesh.

  With respect to the problem of evil, the truth Jung finds latently expressed in Job is that we can no longer accept the pious maxim that "all good is from God and all evil from man." Tracing his argument through the story of Eden, Job, myths about Satan as God's fallen son, and the portrait of Christ uttering his cry of dereliction on the cross, Jung contends that these hints from the unconscious suggest that another perspective on evil is needed, one that does greater justice to the experience, recognized by the unconscious but too repugnant for consciousness to acknowledge, that both in the "life of God" and in the biography of humans, there is a mysterious interplay between good and evil, light and darkness, grace and judgment. With obvious reference to the Holocaust, Jung proposes that the question of the "good God" in the face of such evil is "burningly topical," to which theologians and laypersons alike might make a contribution; cf. *CW* XI, "Answer to Job," p. 453.

  With respect to the concept of God as present in human flesh, Jung observes that as easy as we find it today to acknowledge the doctrine of the incarnation as applying to Jesus of Nazareth two thousand years ago, we find it much more difficult to take seriously the hints in Scripture that we are born in God's image, that we are one with God, and that we are God's temples with his spirit dwelling within. Jung adverts to the mystical intuition of Meister Eckhardt who speaks of the need for God to "be born in the human soul;" cf. *CW* XI, p. 456. Admitting such a thought to consciousness by no means exempts us from a sense of complicity with evil, given the numinous interplay between good and evil everywhere, as noted above. What such insight achieves is the heightening of awareness, on the one hand of the real power for darkness that resides in each of us, but on the other, of the God-given presence within that can strive to mitigate such evil and undermine its power. Admitting such awareness to consciousness would, in Jung's judgment, have profound impact on our sense of moral responsibility in the modern world.

26. *CW* XI, "Answer to Job," pp. 362–3.
27. Ibid., p. 456.
28. "Psychology and Alchemy," *CW* XII, pp. 10 f. I am indebted to Bayard P. Herndon, whose doctoral dissertation at the Hartford Seminary Foundation in 1978 on *The Problem of Transcendence in the Thought of Edmund Husserl, Maurice Merleau-Ponty, Rudolf Bultmann, and Carl Gustav Jung*, sets forth his thesis on the need to recast our concept of transcendence from a transcendence "above" to a transcendence "below" or "within."
29. *CW* XI, "Answer to Job," p. 360.
30. Ibid., p. 361.

Chapter IV: Biblical Symbols: The Vocabulary of the Soul

1. *M&S*, p. 21.
2. Robert E. Luccock, ed., *Halford Luccock Treasury* (Nashville: Abingdon, 1963), pp. 160f.
3. *M&S*, p. 21.
4. Jacobi, *Complex, Archetype, Symbol*, p. 80, citing Jung.
5. C. H. Dodd, *The Parables of the Kingdom* (New York: Charles Scribner's Sons, 1958), p. 16.
6. Philipson, op. cit., p. 71, citing Jung.
7. 1 Corinthians 1:17; Colossians 1:20; 2:14.
8. Isaiah 40:22; Ecclesiastes 1:6; Psalm 19:6.
9. See the description of the city as a perfect square, Revelation 21:12–21.
10. *CW* X, "Flying Saucers: A Modern Myth," p. 409.
11. See the transfiguration narrative in Mark 9:2–13 and parallels, where Jesus appears to be the new "third" product of two preceding traditions, *viz.*, law (Moses) and prophecy (Elijah).

12. Cf. John A. Sanford, *The Kingdom Within* (Philadelphia: J. B. Lippincott Co., 1970), p. 179, citing *The City of God*, XI. xxx and *On Christian Doctrine*, II. 39. For a contemporary perspective on scriptural numerology see Marvin Pope, "Numbers," *The Interpreter's Dictionary of the Bible* (Nashville: Abingdon, 1962), Vol. K-Q, pp. 564–7; "Seven," *IDB*, Vol. R-Z, pp. 294–5; "Twelve," ibid., p. 719.
13. *CW* XIV, "Mysterium Coniunctionis," p. 248.
14. R. W. Corney, "Color," *IDB*, Vol. A-D, p. 657.
15. *CW* XI, "Psychology and Religion," p. 39.
16. Cf. V. H. Kooy, "Symbol, Symbolism," *IDB*, Vol. R-Z, pp. 472–6.
17. Hicks painted more than sixty versions of this scene, finding in it a powerful symbol of what Jung called the "conjunction of opposites" or what in biblical terms might be called reconciliation. For Hicks the animals symbolically expressed the peace-making taking place within society between the white settlers and the native Americans, portrayed in the corner of each of his paintings by the image of William Penn making peace with the Delaware Indians. Hicks also saw the animals as symbols of the "conjunction of opposites" within the self. In a sermon Hicks compared the animals to the four "humours," the wolf = avarice, the leopard = the sanguine, the bear = the phlegmatic, and the lion = the choleric. Hicks concluded his sermon, "May the melancholy be encouraged and the sanguine quieted. May the phlegmatic be tendered and the choleric humbled. May self be denied and the cross of Christ worn as a daily garment; may his peaceable kingdom forever be established in the rational immortal soul." Cf. *Time* (May 19, 1975), pp. 62–3.
18. *MDR*, p. 42.
19. The one scriptural exception to the rule that "no one has seen God" is found in Exodus 33:20–23, where Moses is permitted briefly to see God's "back" as he passes before Moses; cf. also Genesis 16:13; 32:30; Exodus 24:10.
20. *MDR*, p. 140.
21. B. Herndon, op. cit., p. 366.
22. Jacobi, *Complex, Archetype, Symbol*, p. 78, quoting Goethe.
23. Schaer, *Religion and the Cure of Souls in Jung's Psychology*, p. 161, citing Jung.
24. *CW* X, "The Undiscovered Self," p. 279.

Chapter V: Biblical Archetypes and the Story of the Self

1. *CW* XV, "On the Relation of Analytical Psychology to Poetry," p. 82.
2. Campbell, op. cit., pp. xxx–xxxi. Jung was not the first to take note of these stereotypical images, but he was the first to make their investigation a paramount concern; cf. *M&S*, pp. 67f.

3. *M&S,* p. 67.
4. Ibid., p. 69. Another type of example is the young female subject Jung describes in his doctoral dissertation on "The Psychology and Pathology of the So-Called Occult Phenomena." In a state of trance the girl reported a vision of the cosmos that bore remarkable resemblance to the cosmogonic descriptions produced by the Christian Gnostics of the second century A.D. Cf. *CW* I, pp. 39–42.
5. *CW* XI, "Psychology and Religion," p. 103.
6. *CW* III, "Schizophrenia," pp. 261–2.
7. See *Jacobi,* pp. 39–41; Campbell, op. cit., p. xiii.
8. From "Liber de diversis quaestionibus," XLVI; cf. *Jacobi,* pp. 39–40.
9. Calvin S. Hall and Vernon J. Nordby, *A Primer of Jungian Psychology* (New York: New American Library, 1973), p. 42, quoting Jung, *CW,* IX.1, p. 79.
10. Philipson, op. cit., p. 58.
11. *Jacobi,* p. 41, quoting Jung.
12. *M&S,* p. 75.
13. Jacobi, *Complex, Archetype, Symbol,* pp. 45f.
14. *M&S,* p. 79.
15. *Jacobi,* p. 40.
16. Philipson, op. cit., pp. 62f., quoting Jung.
17. *CW* IX.1, "The Psychology of the Child Archetype," pp. 162–3.
18. *M&S,* p. 89.
19. Philipson, op. cit., p. 59, quoting Jung.
20. *CW* IX.1, "The Concept of the Collective Unconscious," p. 48.
21. Joseph Campbell, *The Hero with a Thousand Faces* (Cleveland: World Publishing Co., 1956).
22. Adapted from Maude Barrows Dutton, *The Tortoise and the Geese and Other Fables of Bidpai* (Boston: Houghton and Mifflin, 1908), pp. 84–89.
23. Peter Jenkins, *A Walk Across America* (New York: Fawcett Crest, 1979), p. 143.
24. In a sense the "hero archetype" has more to do with *process* than *person* insofar as it reflects an aspect of the process of individuation.
25. *MDR,* pp. 196, 199.
26. David Cox, *Modern Psychology: The Teachings of Carl Gustav Jung* (New York: Barnes and Noble, 1968), p. 153.
27. Edward F. Edinger, *Ego and Archetype* (New York: Penguin Books, 1973), p. 3.
28. Ibid.
29. Wehr, op. cit., p. 49.
30. *CW* XI, "Answer to Job," p. 459.
31. *CW* IX.2, "Christ, a Symbol of the Self," p. 37.
32. *CW* XI, "Answer to Job," p. 441.
33. *CW* IX.2, "Christ, a Symbol of the Self," p. 40.

34. Ibid., p. 38.
35. Cf. excerpt in Wayne Meeks, *The Writings of Paul* (New York: W. W. Norton, 1972), pp. 268–70. Eugene TeSelle, *Christ in Context* (Philadelphia: Fortress Press, 1975) presents a chapter on "The Archetype Christology" of Kant, Schleiermacher, and Hegel, pp. 47–126. Cf. also Robert Detweiler, who discusses "the Christ figure as mythological archetype" in "Christ and the Christ-Figure in American Fiction," reprinted in *New Theology No. 2*, ed. M. E. Marty and D. G. Peerman (New York: Macmillan, 1965), pp. 302–4.
36. Early Christians adopted the title "the Way" to describe themselves, probably prior to their using the term "Christian" (Acts 9:2; 22:4; 24:14).
37. *CW* V, "Symbols of Transformation, Part One," pp. 69–70.
38. *CW* XV, "On the Relation of Analytic Psychology to Poetry," p. 82.

Chapter VI: Letting the Bible Speak: A Jungian Approach to Biblical Interpretation

1. *CW* X, "After the Catastrophe," p. 217.
2. Henri Nouwen, *The Wounded Healer* (New York: Doubleday, 1972), pp. 25f.
3. One of the key developments in New Testament studies in the past decade is a structuralist analysis of the biblical text. Though structural exegesis does not penetrate as far as Jung in examining "the manner in which aspects of meaning are produced and apprehended by the human mind," it has taken giant steps in drawing the attention of biblical scholars to the "symbolic or connotative dimensions" of a text, its "power" and its "deep values" that have "the power of transforming unreality into reality" for the reader. Cf. Daniel and Aline Patte, *Structural Exegesis: From Theory to Practice* (Philadelphia: Fortress Press, 1978) as well as the *Semeia* series of Fortress Press and Scholar's Press.
4. Andrew Miles, O.S.B., "Understanding God's Word," *The Pecos Benedictine* (October 1978), pp. 2,7.
5. Revelation 22:18–19 is the only New Testament passage that holds individual words sacrosanct and inviolable (though cf. Deut. 4:2; 12:32). The Apocalypse stands at the opposite pole from Paul who maintains that the "letter kills" (2 Cor. 3:6).
6. See the excellent overview of the use of the concept "Word of God" in Scripture in John Reumann, *Jesus in the Church's Gospel* (Philadelphia: Fortress Press, 1968), pp. 18–21.
7. *CW* XI, "Answer to Job," pp. 412–13.
8. Thomas Merton, *Opening the Bible* (Collegeville, MN: Liturgical Press, 1970), p. 28.

9. *MDR*, p. 340.

10. Merton, op. cit., p. 19.

11. Ibid., p. 25.

12. Cf. Ernst Käsemann, *Perspectives on Paul* (Philadelphia: Fortress Press, 1971), p. 35.

13. *CW* X, "Flying Saucers: A Modern Myth," p. 410.

14. *Jacobi*, p. 86.

15. *MDR*, p. 391.

16. Hall and Nordby, op. cit., p. 112.

17. *CW* XV, "On the Relation of Analytical Psychology to Poetry," p. 74.

18. Philipson, op. cit., p. 65, n. 36, citing Jung.

19. *CW* VIII, "The Transcendent Function," pp. 77–91.

20. Ibid., p. 86.

21. Bennet, op. cit., p. 112.

22. Ibid., pp. 107–8.

23. Bennet, op. cit., pp. 109–110.

24. James Hillman, *The Myth of Analysis* (Evanston, IL: Northwestern University Press, 1972), p. 189, citing *Confessions* X. 8.

25. *Jacobi*, p. 86.

26. Mark Link, S. J. *You: Prayer for Beginners and Those Who Have Forgotten How* (West Los Angeles, CA: Argus, 1976), pp. 36–37.

27. *CW* XVI, "Principles of Practical Psychotherapy," p. 8; cf. also, *MDR*, pp. 132f.

28. M. Basil Pennington, O. C. S. O., *Daily We Touch Him* (Berkeley, CA: Image Books, 1979), pp. 33–41.

29. See for example, N. D. McCarter, *Help Me Understand, Lord: Prayer Responses to the Gospel of Mark* (Philadelphia: Westminster Press, 1978); the New Testament commentary series *Pray and Read* (Chicago: Franciscan Herald Press); National Catholic Reporter cassette tape by Eugene LaVerdiere, *Praying with the Scriptures;* George Martin, *Reading Scripture as the Word of God* (Ann Arbor, MI: Word of Life, 1975).

30. Martin, op. cit., p. 85.

31. Cf. for example, John Reumann, "Methods in Studying the Biblical Text Today," *Concordia Theological Monthly,* XL (1969), pp. 655–81, who writes that in preaching, one must ultimately "consider whether a given passage is relevant even if it be treated allegorically or typologically." As another instance, cf. Raymond E. Brown, *The Gospel According to John, I-XII,* Vol. 29, Anchor Bible (New York: Doubleday & Co., 1966) who notes Rudolf Bultmann's allegorical or symbolic interpretation of the "beloved disciple" figure, oddly paralleling the hermeneutics of Gregory the Great who offered a similar interpretation, pp. xciv f. Brown himself in discussing John 1:51 recommends that "we must look for a figurative meaning" (p. 89).

32. The author of Hebrews uses allegory explicitly in interpreting the Isaac story "figuratively" *(en parabolē)* as an account of receiving someone back from the dead. Paul engages in allegory (Gal. 4:24) and typology (Rom. 5:18). Cf. the typological comparison of Noah's deliverance with the rite of baptism (1 Pet. 3:20f.) and of Melchizedek to Christ (Heb. 7:1–17).

Chapter VII: God, the Bible, and the Self in Jungian Perspective

1. *MDR,* p. 40.
2. Ibid., p. xi.
3. *M&S,* p. 101.
4. Schaer, *Religion and the Cure of Souls,* p. 127.
5. See the discussion of Jung's use of Scripture in chapter I.
6. *M&S,* p. 101.
7. Samuel Sandmel, *The Hebrew Scriptures* (New York: Knopf, 1963), p. 3.
8. C. G. Jung, *Psychological Reflections: An Anthology of Jung's Writings,* ed. Jolande Jacobi (New York: Pantheon Books, 1953), p. 343.
9. *MDR,* p. 44.
10. Ibid., pp. 44–5.
11. Ibid.
12. Ibid., pp. 74–5.
13. Ibid., p. 45.
14. Ibid., p. 150.
15. *CW* XI, "Psychology and Religion," p. 5.
16. Wehr, op. cit., p. 86.
17. *CW* XII, "Introduction to the Religious and Psychological Problems of Alchemy," p. 13.
18. *CW* X, "The Undiscovered Self," p. 280.
19. *MDR,* pp. 138–140.
20. *M&S,* p. 87.
21. C. G. Jung, *Modern Man in Search of a Soul* (New York: Harcourt, Brace, 1933), p. 229.
22. *CW* XI, "Psychology and Religion," p. 8.
23. *CW* XII, "Introduction to the Religious and Psychological Problems of Alchemy," p. 12.
24. Wehr, op. cit., p. 111; *MDR,* p. 86.
25. Wehr, op. cit., pp. 111–12.
26. *CW* X, "The Undiscovered Self," pp. 256–62.
27. Jacobi, *Complex, Archetype, Symbol,* p. 105.
28. *CW* XI, "Psychology and Religion," pp. 104–5.
29. Bennet, op. cit., p. 167.
30. Ibid., pp. 167–9.

31. Van der Post, *Jung and the Story of Our Time,* adds personal vignettes that amplify these two publications.
32. *MDR,* p. 43.
33. Ibid.
34. Ibid., p. 53.
35. Ibid., p. 69.
36. Ibid., p. 63.
37. Ibid., pp. 53–55.
38. Ibid., p. 55.
39. Ibid., p. 75.
40. Ibid., p. 40.
41. Ibid., p. xi.
42. Ibid., p. 92.
43. *CW* XI, "Answer to Job," p. 361.
44. *CW* X, "The Meaning of Psychology for Modern Man," p. 155; *CW* XI, "Answer to Job," pp. 361–2.
45. *CW* VIII, "On Psychic Energy," p. 55.
46. *MDR,* p. 56.
47. *CW* XI, "Answer to Job," p. 358.
48. Edinger, op. cit., p. 101.
49. *MDR,* pp. 66–7.
50. Ibid., pp. 77–8.
51. Ibid., p. 72.
52. *CW* XII, "Introduction to the Religious and Psychological Problems of Alchemy," pp. 10f.
53. *CW* X, "The Undiscovered Self," pp. 293–4.
54. *CW* XII, "Introduction to the Religious and Psychological Problems of Alchemy," p. 11, n. 6.
55. Schaer, op. cit., pp. 149–50.
56. Ibid., p. 152.
57. Ann and Barry Ulanov, *Religion and the Unconscious* (Philadelphia: Westminster, 1975), p. 91.
58. *MDR,* p. 40.
59. Cited in Aniela Jaffé, ed., *C. G. Jung: Word and Image,* Bollingen Series, XCVII:2 (Princeton: Princeton University Press, 1979), pp. 138–39.

Epilogue: Psychological Criticism and Scriptural Studies

1. *MDR,* p. 326.
2. See the reference to F. C. Grant's call for a "psychological criticism" in the preface. In 1953 Henry Cadbury stated that so many of the issues in biblical interpretation are fundamentally "psychological rather than literary. . . . It is regrettable," he comments, "that so little has been done

and is being done to match the study of expression with a study of mind and experience" (*Harvard Divinity School Bulletin*, XIX, 1953, p. 54). More recently, Peter Stuhlmacher in *Historical Criticism and Theological Interpretation of Scripture* asks if, "we actually need additional psychological and sociological . . . categories and methods of interpretation to broaden and give precision to our understanding of tradition" (Philadelphia: Fortress Press, 1977), p. 86.

3. "On the Relation of Analytical Psychology to Poetry," in Campbell, *Portable Jung*, pp. 302 ff.
4. Neusner, op. cit., p. 113.
5. "On Wrestling with God: Using Psychological Insights in Biblical Study," *Religion in Life*, XLVII, 1978, p. 142.
6. "Perspectives and Methods in Contemporary Biblical Criticism," *Biblical Research*, XXII, 1977, p. 45.
7. Cf., Francoise Dolto and Gerard Séverin, *The Jesus of Psychoanalysis*, tr. Helen R. Lane (Garden City, New York: Doubleday and Co., 1979), which on the whole imposes Freudian models of interpretation on the text, but on occasion provides original and compelling insight into the dynamics of biblical story, as for example, in their treatment of the story of the Wedding at Cana, pp. 54–70. The volume demonstrates the need for background in biblical exegesis, which is lacking almost completely. In contrast, see the durable work of Robert Leslie, *Jesus and Logotherapy* (New York: Abingdon, 1965), which blends biblical critical sophistication with analytic insight from the standpoint of the existential psychotherapy of Viktor Frankl.
8. "Psychology as a Tool to Interpret the Text," *Christian Century* (March 24, 1982), p. 336.
9. Smith, op. cit.

Select Bibliography

I. The Writings of C. G. Jung

Analytical Psychology, Its Theory and Practice (The Tavistock Lectures). Foreword by E. A. Bennet. New York: Pantheon, 1968.

C. G. Jung Letters, I–II. Edited by Gerhard Adler and Aniela Jaffé. (Bollingen Series XCV. Princeton: Princeton University Press, 1973–75.

The Collected Works of C. G. Jung. Edited by Gerhard Adler, Michael Fordham, Sir Herbert Read, and William McGuire. Translated by R. F. C. Hull. Vols. I–XX. Bollingen Series XX. Princeton: Princeton University Press, 1953–78. *The following essays have special relevance for students of religion and Scripture:*

Vol. IX.1   "The Psychology of the Child Archetype"
Vol. IX.2   "Christ, a Symbol of the Self"
            "Background to the Psychology of Christian Alchemical Symbolism"
            "Gnostic Symbols of the Self"
Vol. X   "The Spiritual Problem of Modern Man"
            "The Meaning of Psychology for Modern Man"
            "The Undiscovered Self"
Vol. XI   "Psychology and Religion" (The Terry Lectures)
            "A Psychological Approach to the Dogma of the Trinity"
            "Transformation Symbolism in the Mass"
            "Psychoanalysis and the Cure of Souls"
            "Answer to Job"
Vol. XII   "Introduction to the Religious and Psychological Problems of Alchemy"
            "Religious Ideas in Alchemy"
Vol. XV   "On the Relation of Analytical Psychology to Poetry"

Man and His Symbols. New York: Doubleday & Co., 1971. Introductory essay by Jung: "Approaching the Unconscious."

Memories, Dreams, Reflections. Edited by Aniela Jaffé. Translated by R. and C. Winston. New York: Pantheon, 1963.

II. *Introductory Interpretive Works*

Hall, Calvin S. and Nordby, Vernon, J. *A Primer of Jungian Psychology.* New York: New American Library, 1973.

Jaffé, Aniela, ed. *C. G. Jung: Word and Image.* Bollingen Series XCVII:2. Princeton: Princeton University Press, 1979. Photographs and quotations from the life and works of Jung.

Jacobi, Jolande. *Complex, Archetype, Symbol in the Psychology of C. G. Jung.* Translated by Ralph Manheim. Bollingen Series LVII. Princeton: Princeton University Press, 1959.

Jacobi, Jolande. *The Psychology of C. G. Jung.* New revised edition. New Haven: Yale University Press, 1971. The standard introduction to the thought of C. G. Jung.

Philipson, Morris. *Outline of a Jungian Aesthetics.* Evanston, IL: Northwestern University Press, 1963. An application of Jung's thought to the task of literary interpretation.

Schaer, Hans. *Religion and the Cure of Souls in Jung's Psychology.* Translated by R. F. C. Hull. Bollingen Series XXI. New York: Pantheon, 1950.

Wehr, Gerhard. *Portrait of Jung: An Illustrated Biography.* Translated by W. A. Hargreaves. New York: Herder and Herder, 1971.

Index of Names and Subjects

Index of Biblical References